DEVIL'S ADVOCATES

DEVIL'S ADVOCATES is a series of books devoted to exploring the classics of horror cinema. Contributors to the series come from the fields of teaching, academia, journalism and fiction, but all have one thing in common: a passion for the horror film and a desire to share it with the widest possible audience.

'The admirable Devil's Advocates series is not only essential – and fun – reading for the serious horror fan but should be set texts on any genre course.'
Dr Ian Hunter, Reader in Film Studies, De Montfort University, Leicester

'Auteur Publishing's new Devil's Advocates critiques on individual titles... offer bracingly fresh perspectives from passionate writers. The series will perfectly complement the BFI archive volumes.' **Christopher Fowler,** *Independent on Sunday*

'Devil's Advocates has proven itself more than capable of producing impassioned, intelligent analyses of genre cinema... quickly becoming the go-to guys for intelligent, easily digestible film criticism.' *Horror Talk.com*

'Auteur Publishing continue the good work of giving serious critical attention to significant horror films.' *Black Static*

 DevilsAdvocatesbooks

DevilsAdBooks

Also available in this series

Antichrist Amy Simmons

Black Sunday Martyn Conterio

Carrie Neil Mitchell

The Curse of Frankenstein Marcus K. Harmes

The Descent James Marriot

Halloween Murray Leeder

Let the Right One In Anne Billson

Nosferatu Cristina Massaccesi

Saw Benjamin Poole

The Silence of the Lambs Barry Forshaw

Suspiria Alexandra Heller-Nicholas

The Texas Chain Saw Massacre James Rose

The Thing Jez Conolly

Witchfinder General Ian Cooper

Forthcoming

Cannibal Holocaust Calum Waddell

Frenzy Ian Cooper

Near Dark John Berra

Psychomania I.Q. Hunter & Jamie Sherry

DEVIL'S ADVOCATES

DEAD OF NIGHT

JEZ CONOLLY AND
DAVID OWAIN BATES

auteur

Acknowledgments

We would like to thank a number of people for the help, interest and encouragement that they gave during the preparation of this book: Caroline Conolly, Dom Fripp, Joanna Hill, Andy Kershaw, Wendy Klein, Kathryn McKee, Nick Riddle, Barbara Roden and Matthew Sweet. Thanks also, as ever, to John Atkinson at Auteur for creating the *Devil's Advocates* series and for providing us with the chance to explore the dusty attic of our *Dead of Night* memories. Thanks to Emily Unthank and the Henry Moore Foundation, for permission to reproduce 'Figure in a Shelter'. Finally very special thanks to Simon Relph for allowing us to reproduce so many of his father's beautiful set design drawings in this book.

First published in 2015 by
Auteur, 24 Hartwell Crescent, Leighton Buzzard LU7 1NP
www.auteur.co.uk
Copyright © Auteur 2015

Series design: Nikki Hamlett at Cassels Design
Set by Cassels Design www.casselsdesign.co.uk
Printed and bound by CPI Group (UK) Ltd, Croydon, CR0 4YY

British Library Cataloguing-in-Publication Data
A catalogue record for this book is available from the British Library

ISBN paperback: 978-0-9932384-3-7
ISBN ebook: 978-0-9932384-4-4

CONTENTS

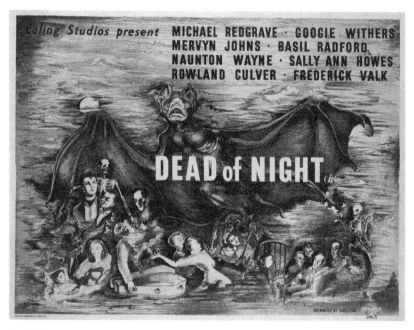

The UK theatrical poster.

INTRODUCTION: 'A WEEKEND IN THE COUNTRY?'

'Pilgrim's Farm...I wonder why that sounds so familiar...'

...on a quiet, sunlit, tree-lined lane in the heart of the Kent countryside a handsome Sunbeam-Talbot 10 cabriolet, registration EYY260, slowly pulls to a halt. Its sole occupant, architect Walter Craig, glances across at the timbered exterior and tiled roof of his destination, Pilgrim's Farm, and a look of puzzlement plays across his face. A look that says, 'Haven't I been here before?'

And so begins (and ends) *Dead of Night*, Ealing Studios' extraordinary post-war treasury of the supernatural. Walter Craig, in the early stages of his *déjà vu* cycle, is about to meet the house guests at Pilgrim's Farm who, upon learning that they are all players in his recurring dream, decide to share recollections of their own strange experiences. Seventy years after its theatrical release, this famously elliptical cinematic anthology of claustrophobic scary stories continues to haunt the dreams of anyone who has seen it. Released a matter of days after the end of the Second World War and a dozen years

ahead of the first full-blooded Hammer horror, it featured contributions from some
of the finest directors, writers and technicians ever to work in British film. Since its
release it has become evermore widely regarded as a keystone in the architecture of
horror cinema, both nationally and internationally, and is regularly cited by writers and
researchers as a singularly important title in the history and development of British
national cinema. Yet for a film that packs such a reputation this, as far as we are aware, is
the first time a single book has been dedicated to its analysis and appreciation.

As is the case with a good number of horror movies made during the pre- and post-
war era, we have television screenings from the 1960s onwards to thank for the kindling
of memories. If you were born in the UK during the period when Amicus Productions
were releasing their succession of lurid portmanteau homages to Ealing's masterpiece
– let's say between 1964 and 1980, roughly the period that demographers and cultural
commentators have come to call 'Generation X' – you probably first discovered *Dead
of Night* tucked away in the twilight zone of the late night television schedules, back in
the days when the midnight movie was followed only by a weather report, a 'good night'
from the announcer, the National Anthem and the ominous black screen and dog-
whistle *ping* of 'Closedown'. *Dead of Night* first did the rounds on regional ITV stations
in the 1960s and 1970s before being picked up by the BBC who proceeded to show it
four times between 1977 and 1990.[1] After these outings it was acquired by Channel 4
who ran the film several times on its main station between 1992 and 2003 and several
times more on its then-pay service FilmFour. It received rather unheralded VHS releases
in 1996 and 1999 before appearing slightly more prominently as part of one of the
Ealing Classics DVD Collection boxsets in 2003, accompanied by *Went the Day Well?*
(Cavalcanti 1942), *Nicholas Nickleby* (Cavalcanti 1947) and *Scott of the Antarctic* (Charles
Frend 1948).

In February 2014 Studio Canal released a digitally restored special edition Blu-ray and
DVD of the film, complete with a 75-minute featurette 'Remembering *Dead of Night*'.
The disc is a fitting and timely celebration of the film, making it widely accessible in the
run-up to its 2015 70th anniversary. In recent times the film featured at number five in
Martin Scorsese's '11 Scariest Horror Movies of All Time', compiled by the director for
The Daily Beast website. A capsule appreciation attributed to Scorsese defines it as 'a
British classic' with a collection of tales that are 'extremely disquieting, climaxing with a

montage in which elements from all the stories converge into a crescendo of madness. It's very playful…and then it gets under your skin' (Scorsese 2009).

Those earlier television screenings were to prove important. In these days of (somewhat ironically) non-stop, round the clock Möbius strip TV schedules that have no discernable beginning or end, or for that matter TV on demand that allows viewers to watch whatever, whenever, it's perhaps a little difficult for children of the eighties and onward to appreciate the early adolescent frisson attached to those fondly remembered opportunities during the pre-VCR Gen X years to stay up long past your bedtime and watch the late film 'live' as it were. In their own small, domestic but quite important way, those viewing opportunities were a pre-teen rite of passage, an early glimpse of a grown-up world beyond midnight. Of the many black and white and often quite whiskery films that the schedulers served up in the wee small hours of our youth *Dead of Night* was one that both authors of this book independently remember very clearly, and yet in the intervening years the specific reasons for its memorable effectiveness have been rather elusive. To quote Walter Craig in his efforts to explain what it's like trying to remember a dream: 'How shall I put it…being out at night in a thunderstorm, there's a flash of lightning, and for one brief moment everything stands out vivid and starkly'. This book is our attempt to capture the film's lightning strike. There's a sense that it was one of those films that lodged itself in a cobwebbed corner of the post-Baby Boomer collective consciousness; conversations that we've had about it with our respective contemporaries in the intervening years have frequently resulted in questions such as 'is that the one with the ventriloquist's dummy?' cropping up, usually followed by a detectable shiver of remembrance.

The measured creep of Walter Craig's car along the lane provides not only a suitably understated opening to *Dead of Night*, but also an indicative speedometer reading of the effect the film will have on its audience. Viewing *Dead of Night* was, still is (and, to borrow the film's narrative structure, will forever be) an experience that results, steadily, gradually, in goose bumps, cold sweat and the prickle of nape hairs. Such physical manifestations of fear, more readily associated with the macabre spine-chilling tales of Sir Arthur Conan Doyle and Edgar Allan Poe, are enduring testament to the film's power to genuinely terrify anyone who watches it.

Modern audiences may struggle to regard *Dead of Night* as a horror film by definition. Perhaps a more appropriate classification would be 'terror film'. If one considers the distinction between terror and horror that emerged in early analyses of Gothic literature, a basic interpretation of *Dead of Night* might place it in the former category. Ann Radcliffe, one of the most influential pioneers of the Gothic novel, contributed an essay entitled 'On the Supernatural in Poetry' to an issue of *The New Monthly Magazine* published in 1826 in which she distinguished between the two concepts: 'Terror and horror are so far opposite, that the first expands the soul, and awakens the faculties to a high degree of life; the other contracts, freezes, and nearly annihilates them' (Radcliffe 1826). This distinction was substantiated further by Devendra Varma, a leading authority on Gothic literature, in his 1957 work *The Gothic Flame*:

> The difference between Terror and Horror is the difference between awful apprehension and sickening realization: between the smell of death and stumbling against a corpse...Terror thus creates an intangible atmosphere of spiritual psychic dread...Horror resorts to a cruder presentation of the macabre. (Varma 1957: 130)

The dark and troubling feelings of déjà vu experienced by Walter Craig throughout *Dead of Night* are clear signifiers of this intangible dread. But a closer consideration of the direction of travel of Craig's narrative and the procession of vignette tales that constitute the film's portmanteau form reveals a journey from nascent abstraction through to stark realisation, from terror to horror. The film received its British theatrical release on the 4th of September 1945 just two days after the final surrender documents were signed by the Japanese signalling the formal end of the Second World War. Less than six months earlier the world had begun to witness the full horrors of the concentration camps via newsreel footage, a point at which, for many on the British home front, the terror that they had experienced in wartime, of impending death from invasion, bombs and poison gas, were horrifically realised and revealed to them on cinema screens in the most resultantly graphic way imaginable.

It has frequently been noted by other critical assessments of the film that despite its proximity to the war *Dead of Night* makes not a single mention of the conflict, odd on the face of it considering that the impression given by the film's five tale-tellers is that their stories took place in the fairly recent past. And yet each story's setting or circumstance suggests that the events depicted are more likely to have taken place pre-1939, or perhaps more appropriately given the film's themes, were set in an alternative reality in which no war took place. For example, the two sports to feature, motor racing and golf, were effectively suspended for the duration of the conflict. In one story we see an affluent couple living a blandly comfortable life in a London of spacious Chelsea apartments and quaint antique shops, not bomb craters and rationing. We are also shown scenes of a Paris nightclub, 'Chez Beulah', frequented by Britons and Americans which, thanks to the date of a document seen on screen, could not have taken place any earlier than February 1938 and therefore depict a time unaffected by the German occupation of the city. There is nothing on the surface to suggest that this is a nation of people still dealing with the austerity and displacement of the Britain of 1945.

However, we should consider the very first image that appears at the film's beginning; *Figure in a Shelter*, a highly characteristic Henry Moore drawing rendered in pencil, wax crayon, coloured crayon, watercolour wash and pen and ink dating from 1941 that can be seen behind the opening titles. Moore's sketches of figures in the subterranean confines of London Underground stations are almost uniquely synonymous with the British home front experience during the war, but more than that, they vividly capture the interrupted passage through sleep that many British people, especially Londoners, endured during the early years of the conflict as a result of Germany's deliberate night time bombing policy.

So the troubled sleep and dreams of Walter Craig are redolent of the fear-defined slumber deprivations of a nation at war, epitomised by the Moore sketch. The *Dead of Night* effect was, still is, one of caliginous disquiet; you don't particularly relish sleep after a viewing, which by any standards is surely the measure of a successful horror film. But there's much more going on in *Dead of Night* besides simple sleep-depriving frights, and that is what this book sets out to identify, analyse and appreciate. The examination of the film will proceed through each of the separate stories in turn and will focus on a number of themes that each episode provokes. These themes may well run through the entire film and occur in several if not all of the individual stories, but each chapter will focus its discussion on a selection of themes which we feel are especially pertinent to the story under scrutiny.

'Mr. Craig has been having the most frightful dreams…' (reproduced by permission of the Henry Moore Foundation)

We will begin with a contextual 'family tree' chapter designed to illustrate the film's antecedents and chart its line of influence. The discussion of *Dead of Night*'s individual stories will begin with the film's frame tale directed by Basil Dearden, now known and accepted widely by its rather utilitarian title 'Linking Narrative', concerning Walter Craig's troubling *déjà vu* experience at Pilgrim's Farm. After parking his car by the side of Pilgrim's Farm, Craig (Mervyn Johns) is met at the farmhouse's wooden picket gate by Eliot Foley (Roland Culver), the owner of the property who has commissioned Craig to conduct some renovation work, and shortly after Foley introduces Craig to his mother (Mary Merrall) and the other guests we come to understand the nature of what is troubling him. This chapter will examine the ways in which the link story succeeds in defining the overall structure of the film and will also consider the relevance of the decision to make its central character an architect.

The next chapter discusses the first of the house guests' stories, 'Hearse Driver' also directed by Dearden. The story is recounted by racing driver Hugh Grainger (Anthony

Baird) who survives a mid-race crash that leaves him hospitalised with head injuries, in the care of Joyce (Judy Kelly) the dedicated nurse and, we soon learn, his future wife. While convalescing Grainger is witness to a strange temporal shift and a bizarre premonition in the form of a Victorian horse-drawn hearse beneath his nursing home room window. The driver of the hearse (Miles Malleson) delivers perhaps the film's most well-known line: 'Just room for one inside, sir'. The chapter will study the significance of the bed as a prime vehicle for scares in horror cinema and explore the potency of stillness and the suspension of time as devices for eliciting those goose bumps.

'Christmas Party', the first of two stories directed by Alberto Cavalcanti, is told from the perspective of teenager Sally O'Hara (Sally Ann Howes) who relates a spooky encounter that she had at a festive gathering. During a game of 'Sardines', after spurning the amorous adolescent advances of fellow partygoer Jimmy Watson (Michael Allan), she finds herself in the high attic reaches of the party's large country house setting where she happens upon a weeping child dressed in Victorian clothes. Sally comforts the child, who identifies himself as Francis Kent, and sings him to sleep before returning to the party downstairs, only then realising that she has just seen a ghost. The chapter focussing on this story will appraise it in relation to the very English tradition of the festive ghost story and will also chart how the rendering of Sally's tale negotiates the territory of adolescent liminality.

The next chapter concentrates on the third story, 'Haunted Mirror', directed by Robert Hamer, which belongs to socialite Joan Cortland (Googie Withers) who tells the group about her husband Peter (Ralph Michael) and his obsession with an antique mirror. Lurking in the dark grandeur of the other room in the mirror is an unseen entity from a bygone age, the spirit of the mirror's murderous former owner Francis Etherington, that preys on Peter's jealousies. The chapter will look in earnest at the British post-war male gender crisis embodied by Peter Cortland and the comparative strength of character displayed by Joan.

The case for the defence of the fourth tale, the frequently maligned 'Golfing Story' directed by Charles Crichton, will be heard in the next chapter; as well as championing this story's inclusion in the film, the chapter will extend the discussion of the changing portrayal of male characters in a post-war world as evidenced by the use of its two male lead actors, Basil Radford and Naunton Wayne playing golf partners George Parratt and Larry Potter, whose frequent pairing in earlier films had come to represent a particular strand of Britishness during wartime.

This scrutiny of the film's position on matters of masculinity will reach its natural culmination in the chapter devoted to discussing *Dead of Night*'s most potent and well-remembered story, 'Ventriloquist's Dummy' directed by Cavalcanti. The peculiar three-way relationship between the ventriloquist Maxwell Frere (Michael Redgrave) his dummy 'Hugo' and rival ventriloquist Sylvester Kee (Hartley Power) raises many fascinating issues, and alongside the discussion of these there will be a look back to the origins of bestowing animacy upon inanimate objects and the relationship this has to the concept of the Uncanny. There will also be room for a consideration of the 'fourth man' in this story, the 'doubting Thomas' psychiatrist Doctor Van Straaten (Frederick Valk) responsible for the telling of the tale and the rational foil to Craig and the other guests throughout the film as they share their respective supernatural experiences.

The distinguishing feature of the titles in the *Devil's Advocates* series is their shared effort to convince the reader that the horror film under discussion is especially worthy of their attention amid the many movies produced within the genre; moreover that it is a film ripe for re-evaluation by those who may have viewed it previously. With the latter in mind some assumption of basic awareness of the film is made at times, although we hope that enough information is provided at the appropriate moments to act as a guide rope for the entirely uninitiated. Whether you are completely new to *Dead of Night* or a seasoned fan of the film, our wish is that you will find enough in what follows to either seek out a first-time viewing opportunity or dust off your copy and watch it again with fresh eyes. Either way, by the end, if there ever is an end to all things *Dead of Night*, we would like to think that you are that little bit closer to knowing just what makes it scary.

'A NIGHTMARE OF HORROR'

'You see, everybody in this room is part of my dream.'

I suppose because we felt we were at the beginning of a new era after the war we were inclined to try out our talents on different sorts of films – things we had never done before. We decided, for instance, that it would be a good idea to make a series of ghost stories, joined by a suitable central story thread which would display the all-round talents of the creative teams we had built up, and it was from this decision that *Dead of Night* was made. (Sir Michael Balcon: *Michael Balcon presents...a Lifetime of Films.* Hutchinson 1969)

In the spirit of the film's temporal trajectory, and before moving on to the discussion of its constituent parts, it is appropriate to consider some past, present and future context. If there is one phrase that repeatedly crops up when today's writers attempt to define *Dead of Night* in their retrospective reviews and appraisals of the film, it would be 'ahead of its time'. The term has become rather commonplace at the populist end of the film journalism spectrum, but in the case of *Dead of Night* the phrase is certainly apposite

15

if one considers its anticipation of post-war British horror cinema. However for all its reputation as a pioneering work of the genre the film is just as much 'of its time' as it is ahead of it.

Later chapters will discuss the element of psychoanalysis found in the film in greater depth, but for now let's just say that 1945 was a big year for Freudianism in film. In some respects it was the point at which film and psychoanalytic theory culminated. In their modern, definable, recognised forms both came into being around 1895, so by the time of *Dead of Night* both had enjoyed parallel fifty-year histories. The leading academic Laura Marcus, in her introductory chapter to *Sigmund Freud's The Interpretation of Dreams: New interdisciplinary essays*, observed: 'Psychoanalysis and cinema emerged in tandem at the end of the nineteenth century – twin sciences or technologies of fantasy, dream, virtual reality and screen memory.' (Marcus 1999: 34) A few short weeks after *Dead of Night*'s September 1945 release cinema audiences found themselves once again on the psychiatrist's couch; following Frederick Valk's mid-European bespectacled Sigmund schtick as the film's sceptical psychiatrist Dr. Van Straaten, both Herbert Lom's Dr. Larsen in *The Seventh Veil* directed by Compton Bennett and, especially, Michael Chekhov's Dr. Brulov in Hitchcock's *Spellbound* (1945) – a film that shares a writer credit with *Dead of Night* in the shape of Angus MacPhail — channelled the founding father of psychoanalysis for their inspiration.

It is important to interrogate that phrase 'ahead of its time' a little further. In many respects *Dead of Night* was more a cinematic pinnacle of a storytelling tradition than a forebear of a new form. It has plenty of antecedents, both literary and cinematic. Fundamentally the frame narrative is a device that dates back to some of the earliest known examples of recorded storytelling, which were frequently collections of even earlier tales originating in oral storytelling cultures. The ancient Egyptian text now known as 'the Westcar Papyrus' has been dated back to around 1800 BC and consists of five tales of magic and miracles. Several Sanskrit epics and fable stories emerged from India in subsequent centuries, including *Baital Pachisi* which was adapted and translated by Sir Richard Francis Burton and published in 1870 for an English readership as *Vikram and the Vampire*. Burton is more renowned for his translation of *One Thousand and One Nights*, one of the most well-known collections of folk tales and, in the form of Scheherazade's nightly storytelling efforts designed to spare her from death by order of the Persian king Shahryar, another early example of the use of a frame narrative.

The form survived and thrived through other literary cultures; *The Decameron*, Giovanni Boccaccio's sprawling collection of novellas from the mid-fourteenth century was shaped by a narrative set in a deserted Tuscan villa where ten people seek refuge from the outbreak of the plague in Florence and pass the time telling tales. Boccaccio's work proved to be a major influence on Geoffrey Chaucer whose Middle English masterpiece *The Canterbury Tales* is a succession of stories shared by pilgrims en route to the shrine of Saint Thomas a Becket. It's no accident that the prime location for the gathering of the storytelling house guests in *Dead of Night* is called 'Pilgrim's Farm'. Another work of Chaucer, *The Legend of Good Women*, consists of nine linked sections, and, whilst told from the same single narrator perspective unlike the multi-teller form of *The Canterbury Tales*, is regarded as an example of the dream vision or *visio* literary device. Centuries before Freud, the Middle Ages was a period that saw great interest in 'oneiromancy' or dream lore, with many written works delving into the attempted interpretation of dreams.

Beyond these early ancestral highpoints of the frame story form there are more direct forerunners to *Dead of Night* to be found in nineteenth-century literature. Jan Potocki's *The Manuscript Found in Saragossa*, written during the time of the Napoleonic Wars, took the device of a frame tale encompassing separate nested stories to the level of puzzle box complexity. There's a 1965 Polish film adaptation of the book, *The Saragossa Manuscript* (Polish: *Rękopis znaleziony w Saragossie*) directed by Wojciech Has that is worth seeking out. Potocki's tale is a literary example of *mise en abyme*, translated literally as 'placed into abyss', a term originating in heraldry to denote a small shield appearing at the centre of a bigger shield. In literature it denotes the accretion of stories within stories, in the case of *Saragossa*, a convoluted miscellany of Gothic, supernatural and occasionally erotic recollections, the 'Russian doll' embedding of tales that can take the reader several stages within its frame story. The Ventriloquist's Dummy episode in *Dead of Night* features the film's only instance of second stage story nesting; after starting out by recalling his first encounter with Maxwell Frere, Van Straaten proceeds to read Sylvester Kee's witness statement which then becomes the vehicle for the story that unfolds. Incidentally a purely visual instance of *mise en abyme* is known as the Droste effect, a fine example of which can be found in *Citizen Kane* (Orson Welles

1941) when towards the end of the film an aging Kane passes between two facing mirrors and we are treated to a never-ending multiplicity of reflected Kanes. We will come on to infinite loops and mirrors later.

Victorian Gothic literature displayed a preoccupation with supernatural events and madness; this was a period that saw the rise of both spiritualism and the early stages of psychoanalysis, which led to a distinct tendency towards morbid eeriness in the fiction of the times. The influence of the work of Edgar Allan Poe throughout the 1840s cannot be understated, and writers such as Sheridan le Fanu, whose 1872 publication *In a Glass Darkly* featured five stories presented as the posthumous papers of an occult detective, lent weight to the genre and led to its embrace by more mainstream authors in the second half of the century. The theory of dreams was an abiding interest of the foremost writer of the age, Charles Dickens. Although 'psychology' as a recognised term defining a field of study was not in use during Dickens' own lifetime, his ideas concerning dreams expressed through his correspondence as well as his fictional work are at times remarkably anticipatory of the findings of Freud. A letter that he wrote to a Dr. Thomas Stone on 2 February 1851, not published until 1938, sets out some of his own theories on the nature of dreams, and in so doing gives clues as to the writer's own use of dreams in his fiction. In the letter he appears convinced of the relative commonality of dreams, which suggests that as a literary device he regarded them as a unifying experience among his readership. When charting this democracy of dreams he gives among his examples a delicious little foretaste of Craig's dream in *Dead of Night*:

> Are dreams so very various and different, as you suppose? Or is there, taking into consideration our vast differences in point of mental and physical constitution, a remarkable sameness to them?... And how many dreams are common to us all... we all say 'this *must* be a dream, because I was in this strange, low-roofed, beam-obstructed place, once before, and it turned out to be a dream'. (Dickens 1851)

It is tempting to regard *Dead of Night* as the great grandchild of *The Haunted House*, an 1859 portmanteau collection of spooky short stories, 'conducted' by Dickens and originally published in the weekly periodical *All The Year Round*, with contributions from, among others, Wilkie Collins and Elizabeth Gaskell. Dickens' tradition of Christmas ghost stories began in 1843 with *A Christmas Carol*, a well-loved tale laden with troubled sleep, spectral visitants and a past/present/future temporal journey for its central character, and a succession of spooky festive novellas followed throughout the 1840s. By the 1850s Dickens' role as managing editor of the journal *Household Words*, superseded by *All The Year Round*, led to further 'framed tales for Christmas', including what became known collectively as *The Haunted House*. Dickens was responsible for the first and last chapters and established the story narrator, a man determined to take up occupancy of a deserted house and spend Christmas there with a group of friends. Each encapsulated tale told from the perspective of his house guests centres on the peculiar happenings within a different room in the house. The very beginning of the opening chapter is quite reminiscent of Craig's approach to Pilgrim's Farm in *Dead of Night*:

Under none of the accredited ghostly circumstances, and environed by none of the conventional ghostly surroundings, did I first make acquaintance with the house which is the subject of this Christmas piece. I saw it in the daylight, with the sun upon it. There was no wind, no rain, no lightning, no thunder, no awful or unwonted circumstance, of any kind, to heighten its effect. More than that: I had come to it direct from a railway station: it was not more than a mile distant from the railway station; and, as I stood outside the house, looking back upon the way I had come, I could see the goods train running smoothly along the embankment in the valley. I will not say that everything was utterly commonplace, because I doubt if anything can be that, except to utterly commonplace people – and there my vanity steps in; but, I will take it on myself to say that anybody might see the house as I saw it, any fine autumn morning. (Dickens 1859: 1)

Dickens' embrace of the supernatural paved the way for the *fin de siècle* Gothic revival of the 1880s and the publication of the late Victorian Gothic novels everybody knows; *The Strange Case of Dr Jekyll and Mr Hyde* (Robert Louis Stevenson 1886), *The Picture of Dorian Gray* (Oscar Wilde 1891), *Dracula* (Bram Stoker 1897), *The Turn of the Screw* (Henry James 1898) and others defined the prevailing mood of social and ethical decline. An honourable mention should also go to Jerome K. Jerome, who provided a parody of the Dickensian Christmas ghost story anthology with his short 1891 collection *Told After Supper*.

The most venerated exponent of supernatural fiction from the first decades of the twentieth century, M. R. James, began having his ghostly short stories published as early as 1895, *National Review* carrying 'Canon Alberic's Scrap-Book' and *Pall Mall Magazine* publishing 'Lost Hearts' in the same year. James, by turns scholar, Fellow, Dean, Tutor and Provost at King's College, Cambridge, read these two stories aloud for the first time on 28th October 1893 at one of the weekly gatherings of King's select Chit-Chat Club. Present at this first reading was one E.F. Benson, who would go on to carve out a reputation as one of the leading purveyors of supernatural short fiction of his time, and upon whose work two of the stories to feature in *Dead of Night* were based. At one stage in the planning of the film some thought went into making James the sole source of the stories that were to be dramatised, and although this didn't happen the combination of old and new source material that would eventually be used bore many of the qualities of his work.

These nineteenth century roots can be spotted on several occasions in *Dead of Night*; they are there in the previous renovation work to Pilgrim's Farm that Craig has been called in to work on, the period horse-drawn hearse present in Grainger's story, the reference to the 1865 Constance Kent murder case in Sally O'Hara's story and the 'curious history' of the mirror in Joan Cortland's story which the antique dealer Mr. Rutherford (Esme Percy) dates back to 1836. The room that Joan's husband Peter sees in the mirror is both recollective and predictive. At the level of the story it recalls the dark and opulent Gothic interior from which the murderous force that seeks to claim Peter emanates. More than that, it is reminiscent of the sets found in the numerous costume melodramas released in the 1940s by Gainsborough Pictures, Ealing's British production studio competitor. Andrew Spicer, in his book *Typical Men*, considered this keyhole view of Gainsborough's popular brooding eroticism to be symbolic of 'Ealing's fear and fascination with its own 'other'' (Spicer 2001: 175). It also offers a glimpse of the Gothic-infused and heavily sexually charged horror that would come to define the output of Hammer Film Productions a dozen years after the release of *Dead of Night*. When Joan invites Peter to tell her exactly what he sees in the mirror his description could almost have come from the set design notes of Hammer's leading production designer Bernard Robinson:

> It's just as it always is. Instead of my bed there's the other bed. I can see it quite clearly. The posts have vine leaves twisted round, with bunches of grapes at the top.

The hangings are dark red silk. The walls are panelled. There's a log fire burning in the grate.

Perhaps the earliest example of the anthology format in cinema would be D.W. Griffith's 1916 silent masterpiece *Intolerance*, although an alternative school of thought would consider this a 'composite film' rather than an anthology insofar as the linking theme of the film's title simply defines the individual stories and does not represent a frame narrative in and of itself. However it demonstrated an appetite among audiences for the segmentation of feature length films, and proved influential among European film-makers. The earliest horror anthology film is generally recognised to be *Unheimliche Geschichten* (trans. 'Uncanny Tales') directed by Richard Oswald in 1919, which consisted of five stories, including adaptations of Poe's 'The Black Cat' and Stevenson's 'The Suicide Club', embedded in a framing narrative set in a book shop. German Expressionist cinema is rightly regarded as the cradle of the horror film genre; *The Cabinet of Doctor Caligari* (Robert Wiene 1920), *The Golem* (Carl Boese, Paul Wegener 1920) and *Nosferatu* (F.W. Murnau 1922) are the landmark productions from the early twenties, but there were other notable German-made anthologies released in this period. Fritz Lang's *Der müde Tod* (trans. 'Weary Death', English language title: *Destiny* 1921) and Leo Birinsky and Paul Leni's *Das Wachsfigurenkabinett* (English language title: *Waxworks* 1924) both weave their linking narratives around three tales.

The European film-makers and actors who graced the classic Hollywood period of the 1930s and 1940s contributed to several early English language 'omnibus' talkies; in 1932 alone Greta Garbo was the star of Edward Goulding's episodic *Grand Hotel*, Josef von Sternberg directed and Marlene Dietrich starred in the picaresque *Shanghai Express* and Ernst Lubitsch was among the directors to contribute one of the eight tales that constituted *If I Had a Million*. A decade later Julien Duvuvier directed two anthology films in close succession: *Tales of Manhattan* in 1942 and *Flesh and Fantasy* the following year. The latter, a trio of supernatural tales – including one based on Oscar Wilde's short story 'Lord Arthur Savile's Crime' – with a link story set in a gentlemen's club, is the more significant forerunner to *Dead of Night*, both structurally and tonally.

Despite overt discouragement from government and censor during the years of the Second World War regarding the making and showing of horror films in Britain, a thin strand of supernatural dramas crept through the 1940s and Ealing Studios contributed to this before it came to make *Dead of Night*. The popular 1941 screen version of Arnold Ridley's play *The Ghost Train*, directed by Walter Forde for Gainsborough Pictures and starring Arthur Askey and Richard 'Stinker' Murdoch was not the first attempt to bring the story to the screen; during his pre-Ealing association with Gainsborough Michael Balcon co-produced two film versions of the play. The first of these, a 1927 silent film directed by Géza von Bolváry, was made in conjunction with UFA, the German studio synonymous with Expressionist cinema and production base for directors such as Lang and Murnau. Both this and the second version, a 1931 talkie also directed by Forde and featuring Angus MacPhail among its small team of writers, ramped up the scares in Ridley's play compared with the relatively comic interpretation of the later Askey version which most people remember.

The Boulting brothers' 1942 film *Thunder Rock*, while not an Ealing production, featured several actors who would go on to appear in *Dead of Night*, specifically Miles Malleson, Frederick Valk and Michael Redgrave who, in his portrayal of David Charleston, a cynical journalist in self-imposed exile at a Lake Michigan lighthouse, displays the levels of sanity-questioning intensity that would come to be associated with his interpretation of the ventriloquist Maxwell Frere. *Thunder Rock*, also based on a stage play, was constructed in large part of flashback episodes detailing the lives of the various ghosts that haunt the lighthouse, the cumulative effect of which serves to convince Charleston of the folly of his isolationist thinking.

The most directly significant predecessor to *Dead of Night* displayed Ealing's understanding of the part that subtle supernatural fantasy could play in pursuit of, if you will, the raising of home front spirits during the war years. *The Halfway House*, released in 1944, was a production that drew together many of the talents at Ealing that would subsequently contribute to the making of *Dead of Night*; the two films share Mervyn Johns and Sally Ann Howes in front of the camera and seventeen crew behind it, including director Basil Dearden, writers Angus MacPhail and T.E.B. Clarke, art director Michael Relph and editor Charles Hasse. The main setting for the film is also reminiscent of Pilgrim's Farm, and while the house of the title is located in the Welsh rather than the Kentish countryside, the two interiors share an ineluctable claustrophobia. Both films are deeply defined by their respective temporal anomalies and disruptions; in *The*

Halfway House the characters who gather at the small hotel of the title come to realise that they have been transported back in time by exactly one year to the point when the place was destroyed by German bombing. The apparent time slip presents them with an opportunity to reflect upon their previous choices and current circumstances, enabling them to face their futures with renewed resolve and courage.

Michael Balcon's expressed wish during the early years of the war was for Ealing to produce as he put it 'films of a character which will be of national use at this time', and by inducting several leading practitioners from the sphere of documentary film-making, including GPO Film Unit acting head Alberto Cavalcanti, into the studio's elite coterie of creatives, he injected a fine-tuned realism that lent veracity to the studio's fictional features. This round table of talents, dubbed 'Mr. Balcon's Academy for Young Gentlemen' by the studio's ebullient publicity director Monja Danischewsky, would bring Balcon's ethos to the screen and frequently collaborate on projects. It is from this cradle of cooperative artistry that *Dead of Night* emerged. Balcon pithily articulated his doctrine in his short paper 'Realism or Tinsel' delivered to the Workers Film Association of Brighton in early 1943. This important document set out his opposition to film as purely escapist entertainment, but more than that, it helped to define the distinction that he saw between cinematic realism and naturalism. Documentarist rigour applied to the telling of fictional stories was what he sought. So a type of poetic realism came to emerge as a characteristic of Ealing's output, a product of the desire to move beyond the more urgently propaganda-driven films of the early 1940s.

There had been a tacit accord between the Ministry of Information, the censor and film-makers in Britain to steer clear of producing horror films during the war years.[2] For all its supernatural themes, *The Halfway House*, being released in 1944, still came wrapped in a propaganda dust jacket, but by the time of *Dead of Night* no such 'National Interest' obligations needed to be observed, indeed as Balcon himself noted in his autobiography the prospect of the aftermath provoked a natural departure from the previous output requirements:

> In the immediate post-war years there was as yet no mood for cynicism; the bloodless revolution of 1945 had taken place, but I think our first desire was to get rid of as many wartime restrictions as possible and get going. The country was tired of

regulations and regimentation, and there was a mild anarchy in the air. (Balcon 1969: 159)

The comedies that Ealing would become renowned for, beginning with *Hue and Cry* in 1947, were without doubt a product of this 'mild anarchy', but the post-war, pre-comedies releases, with *Dead of Night* at the forefront, were the revolutionary vanguard. Not that the studio's films in this period were runaway commercial successes; cinema trade paper *Kine Weekly*'s not-altogether scientific annual round-up of box office highs and lows hardly featured any Ealing films during this period, with the notable exception of *Dead of Night*. Despite the film's comparative popularity, but perhaps also because of the success of the later comedies, the studio was reluctant to commit to further anthology films with any great haste. In fact it took four years and the release of the four-part fateful disaster drama *Train of Events* (Sidney Cole/Charles Crichton/ Basil Dearden 1949) for the next Ealing portmanteau to appear. After *Dead of Night* Balcon's team tended to steer clear of supernatural subject matter by and large, with the exception of *The Night My Number Came Up* (Leslie Norman 1955), a tale of a premonitory dream of a plane crash starring Michael Redgrave. Beyond Ealing, though, there were several other British anthology films made in the post-war years, most prominently the multi-director multi-story trilogy of W. Somerset Maugham adaptations *Quartet* (1948), *Trio* (1950) and *Encore* (1951).

During the decade after *Dead of Night* British cinema may have been dark at times – there were numerous British noir films made in that period, several of which were produced by Ealing – but it rarely delivered full-blown scares. It would take Hammer Films' move into the horror genre for this to recommence, starting with *The Quatermass Xperiment*, Val Guest's 1955 big screen adaptation of Nigel Kneale's television series, and proceeding through and beyond that studio's production line of renowned adaptations of *Dracula*, *Frankenstein* and other increasing gruesome and lurid source material. One non-Hammer, less-widely-seen British film of note in relation to *Dead of Night*, also from 1955, is *Three Cases of Murder*, due largely to the first and last of its three stories. The first, 'In the Picture' directed by one-time Jean Cocteau collaborator Wendy Toye, concerned a museum assistant (Hugh Pryse) consumed by a painting in the collection featuring a house set in a bleak landscape. A strange visitor to the museum (Alan Badel) leads him through the front door of the house to meet his fate. The third,

'Lord Mountdrago' directed by George More O'Ferrall with uncredited help from the segment's star Orson Welles, was based on a Somerset Maugham short story about a politician consulting a psychoanalyst fearing that one of his adversaries is attacking him through a series of dreams.

Twenty years after *Dead of Night* the horror portmanteau format was revived in Britain by Milton Subotsky and Max Rosenberg's Amicus Productions. A string of anthologies were released, beginning with *Doctor Terror's House of Horrors* in 1965 and continuing until *From Beyond the Grave* in 1974, with Subotsky producing one final effort in 1981 in the form of *The Monster Club* for Chips Productions, the company credited, among others, for produced the *Hammer House of Horror* television series around that same time. The Amicus films were enjoyable, low budget, highly derivative fare which arguably owed their existence to *Dead of Night*. Indeed one or two of the stories found in the Amicus output bore a close resemblance to the Ealing film, the most obvious being 'The Gatecrasher' episode in *From Beyond the Grave* in which David Warner buys an antique mirror that is home to a malevolent spirit.

Aside from the Amicus titles the 1960s also saw an international revival of the horror anthology film. Mario Bava's *Black Sabbath* (original title: *I tre volti della paura* trans. 'The Three Faces of Fear') released in 1963 was arguably the most significant, in part as base camp for the emerging *Giallo* genre of Italian erotic horror/crime films, and three decades later as a major story structure influence on Quentin Tarantino's 1994 multi-story *Pulp Fiction*. Also significant was *Kwaidan* (trans. 'Ghost Stories' Masaki Kobayashi 1964) a poetic compendium of four ghostly tales that is rightly regarded as a major influence on the later development of Asian horror cinema.

The perpetual motion of *Dead of Night* can also be spotted repeatedly in American television output during the 1950s and 1960s; several episodes of *Alfred Hitchcock Presents* and *The Twilight Zone* bear remarkable similarities to aspects of the Ealing film. The widespread love of these series led in turn to the production of a brace of Hollywood-made horror anthology homages in the 1980s. *Twilight Zone: the Movie*, co-produced and co-directed by Steven Spielberg in 1983, although flawed is still the most notable example of these. Spielberg, ever striving to bridge the gap between his childhood TV and movie memories and his own output, has one way or another played his part in sustaining the *Dead of Night* lineage; he contributed a story to the feature length portmanteau pilot episode of *Twilight Zone* creator Rod Serling's *Night Gallery* in 1969. He would later work with *Dead of Night*'s cinematographer Douglas Slocombe on *Close Encounters of the Third Kind* (1977) and the first three *Indiana Jones* films and also came close to directing the 1978 screen version of *Magic*, eventually helmed by Richard Attenborough, about a ventriloquist (Anthony Hopkins) controlled by his dummy. Despite missing out on *Magic*, Spielberg managed to squeeze a ventriloquist's dummy with a subversive personality into his messy 1979 comedy *1941*.

In the world of British television humour, certain comedy magpies have plundered elements of *Dead of Night* in recent years, invariably with a warm regard. The 2001 Steve Coogan vehicle *Dr. Terrible's House of Horrible*, aside from its obvious affectionately tongue-in-cheek take on the Amicus anthologies, included an episode, 'And Now the Fearing…', about the trapped occupants of an elevator who swap chilling dream tales before arriving at the thirteenth floor to meet their dreaded fate at the whim of the lift attendant, who signs off with 'Room for more inside, mind the doors please!' The quartet of writers and performers that formed the League of Gentlemen have given a nod to *Dead of Night* on several occasions; their 2000 Christmas Special, with its link story wrapped around three darkly funny tales, owed a great deal to the film. The Mark Gatiss-penned 2008 three-part series *Crooked House* bore the distinct flavour of the Ealing nightmare. Steve Pemberton and Reece Shearsmith's 2014 series *Inside No. 9* featured an episode called 'Sardines', the name of the game played by Sally O'Hara and the other children in *Dead of Night*'s 'Christmas Party', which tells of a growing collection of party guests gradually squeezing into the confined space of a wardrobe. Shearsmith is also one of the enthusiastic talking heads to feature in the Studio Canal DVD and Blu-ray 'Remembering *Dead of Night*' featurette. The non-performing League of Gentlemen member Jeremy Dyson devoted several pages of analysis of the film to his 1997 book *Bright Darkness: the Lost Art of the Supernatural Horror Film*, and *Ghost Stories*, his phenomenally successful stage play co-written with Andy Nyman which premiered in 2010, demonstrated that the long dark shadows cast by *Dead of Night* continue to touch and inspire his creative output.

Past, present, future. Both of its time and ahead of its time. *Dead of Night* is much loved, frequently imitated, never bettered. These are its stories.

'I'VE DREAMT ABOUT YOU OVER AND OVER AGAIN, DOCTOR'

'Everybody dreams, Cobb. Architects are supposed to make those dreams real.'
(Stephen Miles [Michael Caine] to his dream space architect protégé Dom Cobb
[Leonardo DiCaprio] in *Inception*, Christopher Nolan 2010)

'Linking Narrative', directed by Basil Dearden, is considered to be loosely based
on a 1912 short story by E.F. Benson entitled 'The Room in the Tower'. While the
source story's repeating dream motif defined the film's framing mechanism, its theme
of vampirism failed to make it onto the screen, although it might just explain the
presence of a looming, fang-baring vampire bat in *Dead of Night*'s most well-known
poster artwork painted by Leslie Hurry, a monster that is entirely absent in the film.[3]
Nevertheless, the link story that charts Walter Craig's tortuous passage through Pilgrim's
Farm, the scene of his perpetual progressions from the bewildered architect invited
down for a weekend in the country to the cold-blooded killer seeking refuge in the
maddening spiral of the other house guests' stories, presents a monstrous circumstance
that, gradually and horrifyingly, is altogether more frightening than any manifestation
of a monster could ever be. Peter Hutchings, when assessing *Dead of Night* in his
book *Hammer and Beyond: The British Horror Film* regards it as 'a horror film without a
recognisable monster, or rather a film where the monster turns out to be the film itself'
(Hutchings 1993: 36).

Dearden's connective sequences are the firm foundation for the film's deserved
reputation, and the seamless ellipse that they constitute has earned *Dead of Night* a
unique place in cinema history. As a result of an evening spent enjoying the film at one
of their local cinemas in Cambridge, the leading cosmologists Fred Hoyle, Hermann
Bondi and Thomas Gold were inspired to formalise their ideas which would lead to the
publication in 1948 of their proposal of the Steady State Theory, that now-discarded
pre-Big Bang model that attempted to explain the origins of the Universe. 'My God! It's
a cosmology. Maybe there's something in this cyclical cosmology', wrote Hoyle in his
diary after seeing the film, and so was born a theory explaining life, the Universe and
everything all based on a horror film about one man's never-ending nightmare.[4]

When approaching 'Linking Narrative' it is interesting to reflect on the relevance of the house at Pilgrim's Farm with regard to the structure of the whole film, and also the importance of establishing the pivotal character Walter Craig as an architect from the outset. *Dead of Night* is a film that is shaped and defined by its points of entry and departure and by the many thresholds in between. For a film that is all about the relative illogic and seemingly unpredictable convolutions of dreams it is an immaculately and meticulously conceived structure, characterised by the passage between and through the succession of story 'chambers' constructed by its four different directors. The individual sections planned and built by Cavalcanti, Crichton, Dearden and Hamer were buttressed and cemented together by Dearden's link story which, unlike the equivalent framing devices found in the overwhelming majority of the film's many imitators, is equal if not superior in quality to the stories that it surrounds.

'Linking Narrative' succeeds in propelling the viewer through the experience of watching *Dead of Night* by providing passageways that steadily enrich our understanding of Walter Craig's predicament. By the 'end' of his story we will be faced with a dilemma ourselves; is Craig an unwitting hostage to fate and thereby driven to commit a murderous act by forces supernatural, or is the act premeditated and his elaborate *déjà vu* narrative unreliable? Each iteration of the framing device gradually develops his story further and in doing so draws us deeper into the fabric of the film. At some point during each of the five separate tales that the link story envelops we bear witness to a crossing point between realms; in 'Hearse Driver' it is the daylight vista beyond Hugh Grainger's hospital bedroom window, in 'Christmas Party' it is the upper reaches of the country house that Sally O'Hara ascends through in order to arrive at Francis Kent's attic bedroom, in 'Haunted Mirror' it is the other room that Peter Cortland can see when he looks into the mirror, in 'Golfing Story' it is the lake that Larry Potter walks into when committing suicide and in 'Ventriloquist's Dummy' it is the backstage route that Sylvester Kee takes in order to discuss business with Maxwell Frere. In each case they/we pass through into, or at very least catch a glimpse of, a different reality that harbours some supernatural manifestation.

These repeated on-screen instances of looking through or passing through apertures of demarcation between worlds are more than mere plot devices, they serve to explicitly immerse the viewer in much the same way that Craig's link story implicitly carries us through. In a sense the most significant threshold through which viewers of *Dead of*

Night pass is that of the edges of the picture they are watching. One of the film's finest attributes is its ability to immerse the viewer in its succession of episodes and in so doing blur the perimeter between their immediate surroundings and the environment of the scenes that they are watching. If one were looking to identify an early reason for the film's successful efforts to frighten its audience, this highly effective and sustained 'lean-forward moment' immersion beyond the fringes of the film image would be it.

The creation of film set interiors in the 1940s was heavily influenced by the work of the art director Perry Ferguson who, in tandem with cinematographer Gregg Toland, realised the deeply suggestive sets demanded by Orson Welles for *Citizen Kane*. The inclusion of many room ceilings in Kane, frequently captured in frame from a low camera perspective, added a dimensionality to the film rarely seen in earlier cinema and kick-started a near-craze among other film-makers of the forties. Rapidly on-screen ceilings were legion and by the time of *Dead of Night*'s making Ealing's output was certainly reflecting this. 'Linking Narrative' director Basil Dearden began his working relationship with *Dead of Night*'s art director Michael Relph in 1943 on the film *The Bells Go Down* which would prove to be the beginning of a collaboration that lasted thirty years. Relph began his career a decade earlier at the age of 17 as assistant art director to Alfred Junge at Gaumont British, then headed by Michael Balcon. Junge developed his expressionist approach to art direction during his time at Berlin's UFA Studios in the 1920s. This together with his involvement in theatre production design rubbed off on the young Relph, who would himself gain experience in theatre design in the 1930s, a skill which benefited his later collaborations with Dearden. The interiors designed by Relph for the Dearden-directed *The Halfway House*, featuring carefully lit and shot low timbered ceilings, displayed the designer's skill at creating spaces capable of instilling confined unease, a quality that was ramped up ten fold for his work on *Dead of Night*.

The sets that feature, particularly the increasingly claustrophobic interior of Pilgrim's Farm, are hugely important to the aesthetic success of the film, and much of this is captured beautifully in Relph's set design drawings, a number of which are reproduced in this book. Much of the *mise-en-scène*, the sets certainly but also the apparatus of fear from the hearse to the mirror to the dummy, are consistent with the concept of the Uncanny. Freud, in his renowned 1919 essay on the subject, defined the Uncanny as 'that class of the frightening which leads back to what is known of old and long familiar'

(Freud 2003: 340). The German term 'unheimlich', coined originally by the psychiatrist Ernst Jentsch in his 1906 essay 'On the Psychology of the Uncanny', translates literally as 'unhomely', an implied association with domestic place that Anthony Vidler picked up on in his 1992 book *The Architectural Uncanny: essays in the modern unhomely*:

> As a concept the Uncanny has, not unnaturally, found its metaphorical home in architecture: first in the house, haunted or not, that pretends to afford the utmost security while opening itself to the secret intrusion of terror, and then in the city, where what was once walled and intimate...has been rendered strange by the spatial incursions of modernity. In both cases of course the uncanny is not a property of the space itself nor can it be provoked by any particular spatial conformation; it is, in its aesthetic dimension, a representation of a mental state of projection that precisely elides the boundaries of the real and the unreal in order to provoke a disturbing ambiguity, a slippage between waking and dreaming. (Vidler 1992: 11)

In the early decades of cinema's rise as a creative medium cultural critics were quick to spot the parallels between film and architecture. Walter Benjamin's highly influential 1936 essay 'The Work of Art in the Age of Mechanical Reproduction' considered the commonalities of aesthetic response between the two; he regarded the dynamism of the moving image, in developing the mass audience as 'distracted examiners', as analogous to the tactile nature of the built environment. Film theorist Peter Wollen attempted to draw out Benjamin's comparison in one of the chapters of his book *Paris Hollywood: Writings on Film*:

> What [Benjamin] wanted to argue was that cinema and architecture both required a kind of kinaesthetic habit formation, the acquisition of a habitual mode of moving through space in order to understand and inhabit it unconsciously. Watching a film, Benjamin believed, was much like moving through a building or a built environment. It required a sense of direction, an attentiveness to signs, an awareness of the purposes for which a place was intended and how it could be most efficiently used. In this sense, architecture and cinema both provide sets of places and spaces which the user must learn how to travel through. (Wollen 2002: 200-201)

The award-winning French architect Jean Nouvel, among other luminaries in his field, has acknowledged the significance of cinema in the formation of his approach to architecture. In an interview quoted in Kester Rattenbury's essay 'Echo and Narcissus' published in a special issue of the journal *A.D., Architectural Design*, Nouvel said:

> Architecture exists, like cinema, in the dimension of time and movement. One conceives and reads a building in terms of sequences. To erect a building is to predict and seek effects of contrast and linkage through which one passes... In the continuous shot/sequence that a building is, the architect works with cuts and edits, framings and openings... I like to work with a depth of field, reading space in terms of its thickness, hence the superimposition of different screens, planes legible from obligatory joints of passage which are to be found in all my buildings... (Rattenbury 1994: 35)

It's not unusual to find film-makers with a past in architecture; Fritz Lang for example, whose father was an architect and construction company manager, studied civil engineering in Vienna before embarking on his directing career after the First World War, a background that can be seen clearly in his 1927 silent masterpiece, *Metropolis*. After an abortive stab at law, *Dead of Night*'s Cavalcanti chose to study architecture in Switzerland, a career path which led him to work in Paris at the age of 18. The move would eventually result in his association with the French avant garde film movement.

Craig's first sight of Pilgrim's Farm from the driver's seat of his car suggests that he is approaching a substantial but fairly unremarkable dwelling.[5] Despite its apparent age the external impression of the building hardly conforms to the Gothic convention of the 'haunted house'. On the face of it the farmhouse is a perfectly non-threatening rural smallholding set neatly in the gentle folds of the South East English countryside. As witnessed by Craig on that bright, sunlit day – we can assume it's wintertime from the visibly bare branches of the trees and Craig's choice of overcoat – there is no obvious reason why he should find the sight of it so puzzlingly full of foreboding. And yet there is enough in Craig's bewildered reaction to its tranquil normality and pleasant, welcoming aspect to indicate that all is not what it seems. We see only a small number of spaces within the walls of Pilgrim's Farm; scenes are set almost exclusively in the drawing room, with brief glimpses of the hallway and small anteroom where the prescient Craig knows to hang his hat and coat, and fleeting shots up or from the staircase leading to an upper level of the house that we never see.

'Linking Narrative': Pilgrim's Farm interior, scene of Walter Craig's unfolding déjà vu

'Hearse Driver': Doctor Albury's office at the nursing home

'Haunted Mirror': Mr. Rutherford's antique shop where Joan Cortland purchases the mirror

'Haunted Mirror': interior of Peter Cortland's bedroom with mirror visible to right

'Golfing Story': the golf club bar where the deceased Potter first appears to Parratt

'Ventriloquist's Dummy': Maxwell Frere's hotel room

'Ventriloquist's Dummy': prison corridor with Frere's cell door to left

Prison interview room where Dr. Van Straaten first meets Frere

The character of Walter Craig could not be described at the archetypal, perhaps stereotypical, on-screen architect. Although they have appeared reasonably regularly as protagonists, the form and function of architects in films has tended to adhere rigidly to a fairly unadventurous blueprint. Characters have frequently been bestowed with the occupation as a quick means of establishing them as creative yet reliable, establishment figures with the required amount of maverick temperament to propel them through the narrative. The lone visionary that was Howard Roark, played by Gary Cooper and modelled heavily on Frank Lloyd Wright in King Vidor's 1949 screen version of the Ayn Rand novel *The Fountainhead*, would likely rank as the most prominent example. Roark had a dream, but unlike Walter Craig's nightmare of horror, his vision is a reflection of The American Dream. He is the perfect embodiment of the Hero Architect, an idealised and rather anachronistic role recalling history's 'master builders' which, in terms of the modern architect, was defined and disputed by the architectural historian Spiro Kostof as 'the romantic hero struggling against the unheeding forces of philistine society to fulfil his unique and prophetic destiny' (Kostof 1977: 331). Roark and Craig may both deal in destiny but there the similarity ends. Roark is as squarely perpendicular and unbending as his modernist constructions. Craig by comparison has an age-worn, almost gnomish aspect in keeping with the eighteenth-century farmhouse he has been hired to work on.

'We've got several other guests so I've put you in the barn' announces Eliot Foley as he brings Craig into the farmhouse. It's a domestic arrangement with an under-taste of class or cultural division, not one based on his status as an architect – moments later Foley acknowledges Craig's 'trained professional eye' – but more likely associated with Craig's ethnic origins. English literature and culture, including cinema, has a long and sorry history of painting the Welsh as a race of stereotypically superstitious, rusticated, peculiar, mystical individuals, defined by a dark archaism and a not altogether healthy supernatural sensitivity. While not quite fully into the realms of 'Noble Savage' or 'Magical Negro' – if anything those two antiquated and decidedly suspect cultural concepts carry a weak positive charge by comparison – Welsh characters supplied a reliable 'other' to the English orthodoxy. Walter Craig is a comparatively nuanced creation; it's crucial that we warm to his plight from the beginning in order for us to be successfully carried through the film's cloistered structure and extra-chilled when the final act of his repeating nightmare plays out.

Despite its evident inspirational role in the advancing of a once popular theory explaining the origins and working of the Cosmos, the film itself is defined more by its concern with time rather than space. Thematically and tonally, and not a little sociologically, the premise of 'Linking Narrative' at least is reminiscent of J.B. Priestley's 'Time Plays', a series of theatrical works written by the playwright between the early 1930s and the mid-1940s that are linked by their exploration of different temporal phenomena. The first of these, *Dangerous Corner* (1932), concerns a party at a country house during which a chance remark triggers a series of revelations. This disclosure of the various characters' dark secrets is erased when the play ends by returning to its opening scene, identical save for the chance remark which this time goes unsaid, resulting in the 'dangerous corner' being avoided. The more celebrated *Time and the Conways* (1937), in its telling of the fate of a family in the two decades after the First World War, has a similar rerun of its beginning at its end. Another of the plays, *I Have Been Here Before* (1937), as the title suggests, deals with the implications of *déjà vu*.

The preoccupation with gatherings in remote, rural settings – inns, hotels and country houses abound – mixed with the temporal loops and resets suggests Priestley's plays from this period were a significant influence on *Dead of Night*. Their legacy was perhaps even more apparent when one considers Ealing's earlier foray into the supernatural, *The Halfway House*; Dearden's film was a precursor to *Dead of Night* in terms of theme, tone and both technical and acting personnel, but its Welsh country inn setting and narrative step back in time liken it greatly to the playwright's work from this period. Priestley may not have worked directly on *Dead of Night* but the high regard in which he was held at the time together with his existing ties with Ealing can only have made him a major influence on the film. Michael Balcon had produced the film version of Priestley's first novel *The Good Companions* for Gaumont British Pictures in 1933, and director Dearden would collaborate with Priestley on the Ealing screen adaptation of the playwright's *They Came to a City* in 1944, in which Priestley himself had a small on-screen part. That film, predating *Dead of Night* by little more than twelve months, displayed Priestley's idealistic utopian polemic, which is the ingredient that separates his work from *Dead of Night*. Its optimism was a world away from the dark post-war recesses of national uncertainty that characterise the Ealing film.

This uncertainty is a theme that will be picked up later in relation to the house guests' stories, but as applied to 'Linking Narrative' we might consider Craig, an architect at the brink of a period of national reconstruction, and recognise his deep personal uncertainty and palpable fear of the near future as a reflection of the nation doubting its ability to rebuild. Depicting a coalescence of family and community for the national good was the underlying aim of many wartime films, and Craig's arrival at Pilgrim's Farm seems to suggest that a further illustration of a 'hearth and home' gathering of individuals will play out. But Craig's furrowed bewilderment upon first catching sight of the building should signal to us that we are not about to observe a patriotic convergence. As Peter Hutchings asserts, the gathering at the farmhouse 'seems to function as a community in the process of disintegration, caught up as its members are in essentially private fears and memories' (Hutchings 1993: 29).

What we actually observe in 'Linking Narrative' is a fabricated 'family' gathering that begins in the hope of daylight but gradually descends into a darkening, fragmentary state with fear as the only binding force. As night falls and the fate that Craig has been predicting and awaiting becomes a reality the surface tension that has held the party together in the drawing room is ruptured leading to disintegration. In the nightmare whirl that follows the room that has contained the film's protagonists effectively falls away, as though the integrity of the bricks and mortar of Pilgrim's Farm has been compromised. As the house guests' stories collapse around Craig, so do the four walls, floor and ceiling that have contained him.

Despite his attempts to hide within the spaces of the others' stories, Craig's murderous act leads to a mob-driven imprisonment within a cell and a swift 'execution', but he has been trapped within his dream the whole time, and the drawing room of Pilgrim's Farm has served as his place of confinement practically from the outset. Many shots are suggestive of prison bars, from the white picket fence outside Pilgrim's Farm to the shadow cast by the spindles of the chair Craig sits in to the single shot through the balusters of the staircase banister. The book cases, leaded windows and exposed beams of the drawing room only increase the sense of incarceration. Craig attempts an escape of sorts in the aftermath of the 'Haunted Mirror' story, but his companions (captors?) manage to keep him within the holding cell that is the farmhouse. Even when the dream breaks, as the final cell into which he has been thrown dwindles to a small aperture in the centre of the screen, we see Craig back in his bed at home wearing striped pyjamas reminiscent of a prisoner's uniform, intimating that Craig's apparent waking is still no escape.

The many rooms and spaces seen in the stories that 'Linking Narrative' encapsulates are intended as temporary chambers of respite; their contents aren't exactly delivered in the hope of alleviating Craig's fears, if anything they reinforce them, but they do at least distract him from his immediate dread. Ultimately, though, they serve to keep him rooted in the environment of his dream and thereby help to ensure his fateful predictions come to pass. Ironically Craig's best hope of being sprung from the trap is Dr. Van Straaten and his efforts to explain the various supernatural events that are related. One almost feels that if his reason were to win the battle of wits the circle of madness and murder might be broken. We actually see Van Straaten in the role of attempted liberator during his own story, when he calls for a jailer to open Maxwell Frere's cell door in order to intervene in the ventriloquist's attack on his own dummy. In the final part of 'Linking Narrative' Van Straaten accepts Craig's dream, and in that moment he seals his own fate.

Director Dearden and his crew deserve credit for keeping the link scenes engrossing, no mean task considering how dispersed the Pilgrim's Farm sections are throughout the film. They also succeed in delivering a dizzying pay-off that concertinas the previous 100 minutes of the film into just three minutes, presenting an end-piece that contains striking resolutions to some of the featured stories, skewed by the murderer Craig's hectic attempt to evade punishment for his crime. When he loosens his neck tie in order to strangle Van Straaten his grip on sanity also loosens, and his panicked efforts to hide illustrate perfectly the fully insane state that he now inhabits.

That final section of the nightmare contains some of the film's most inventive camerawork and lighting. After a short debate following the telling of Van Straaten's ventriloquist's dummy tale the doctor drops and breaks his spectacles when reaching for a drink. The moment coincides with the farm's power plant expiring, plunging the drawing room into semi-darkness, the flames of the open fire providing the only illumination. 'Blimey, George is dying on us' exclaims Foley, 'George' being the name bestowed on the generator. The breaking of the spectacles, the lights going out and the 'death of a man I've never heard of' ('George') were events that Craig predicted over an hour earlier during the link sequence between 'Hearse Driver' and 'Christmas Party', marking the moment when his dream would become a nightmare.

'It's started' mutters Craig, and he insists on being left alone with Van Straaten. His embrace of the dark madness of his fate begins with a slow, low reverse tracking shot in which initially Craig seems to break the fourth wall by looking at the camera/us when rising from his chair. As the camera retreats, however, and the seated back view of Van Straaten enters the frame we see Craig slowly wheel round behind the seated psychiatrist, remove his neck tie and commit the strangulation that his repeating dream has been building up to. Two brief shots follow, one showing Craig's face pulled into a saucer-eyed mask and under-lit by the flames of the open fire, the other his point of view of Van Straaten in the final seconds of his life, the doctor's face upside down and creased with the violent struggle of his final breaths.

Craig's view of the dying Van Straaten is a fleeting nod to the numerous other point-of-view shots that can be found elsewhere in the film; we have a quick one early on, showing Craig's view of the outside of Pilgrim's Farm from the driving seat of his car. A simple, classic establishing shot of course, but it's a moment of first-person perspective that helps to cement Craig as 'our' set of eyes and lead us to take his side in the ensuing logic-versus-superstition battle of wits – we want to believe *his* eyes, which makes his/our point-of-view at the moment of murder all the more chilling. Several times during the encapsulated stories we are encouraged to see through the eyes of a character and believe what they are seeing; consider Hugh Grainger's view outside of his bedroom window in 'Hearse Driver', Sally O'Hara's glance around the country house attic room in 'Christmas Party', Peter Cortland's glimpse of the other room in 'Haunted Mirror' and Sylvester Kee's spinning, consciousness-loss point of view when he is shot and wounded by Maxwell Frere in 'Ventriloquist's Dummy'. There is a final Craig point-of-view shot, a revolving pan when he is surrounded by the cackling mob of guests at Chez Beulah just before they carry him aloft to meet his ultimate fate.

Craig the architect's 'trained professional eye' is able to detect from the very first moments that the world of his dream is decidedly out of true, and when the dream becomes a nightmare and Craig attempts to escape into the world of the house guests' stories, the built environment dissolves into a helter-skelter of spatial impossibilities within which the other inhabitants are determined to find and punish Craig the murderer. He pops up first in the Christmas Party country house mid-way through a game of hide-and-seek at the foot of the staircase. 'Chop, chop, chop, chop, chop!' chant the children, the last line from the popular singing game 'Oranges and Lemons', a rhyme that recalls the fate of Newgate Prison's death row prisoners and the tolling of the church bells associated with executions. The final decapitation actions of the game are traditionally preceded by the lines 'Here comes a candle to light you to bed, here comes a chopper to chop off your head!'. Exaggerated Dutch angles sloping down severely right to left are used to show the now distorted spaces within the country house, suggesting that Craig has a steep uphill task if he is to escape successfully and that in all probability he will slip back into the clutches of his pursuers.[6] To draw a line along the near 45 degrees of those Dutch angle gradients would be to define a 'bend sinister' forward-slash division, a tilted split-line of demarcation that is hinted at subtly at other points in the film. It is there in the shot through the diagonal of the banister at Pilgrim's Farm. Look also at the two shots of Grainger's bedside clock in 'Hearse Driver'; the hands of the clock at a quarter to ten are reflected as a quarter past four if we think of one as a slanting mirror image of the other. When Peter Cortland unwraps his haunted mirror present he props it on a sofa which gives us a reflected view of Peter and Joan at a similar skewed angle. The pattern on Peter's tie is a diagonal stripe, downwards right to left, from which even in reflection there is no escape; a continuity error (we have to suppose) missed when creating the effect of seeing Peter reflected meant that his mirror-image is the same as our non-reflected view of Peter – the stripes on his tie aren't reversed and also fall right to left.

Craig makes for the upper reaches of the house but halfway up the stairs he breaks off into a room where, in the scramble of story elements, he finds Peter Cortland standing in front of his mirror. The Dutch angle abates temporarily, to be replaced by a visual shimmer, giving the impression that Craig has crossed over and is standing next to Cortland in the strange fluid of 'the other room'. Cortland appears to be dressed in nineteenth-century attire and has a demeanour that implies he has been consumed by the spirit of Francis Etherington. 'Something gone wrong with your plans?' asks Cortland/ Etherington, one murderer to another. The liquid shimmer clears and a rapid camera

'One thing is very vivid and very horrible – I hit Sally savagely, viciously.'

pass 'through' the mirror comes to rest on the fresh and inescapable corpse of Dr. Van Straaten. We cut back to the Dutch angles of the country house environment and the final stages of the children's hide-and-seek count. Sally races upstairs, only to be stopped part-way by Craig who pulls her further up the stairs and into the room that Jimmy Watson led her into during 'Christmas Party'. 'Here he is, up in the lumber room!'[7] cries Sally, only to be knocked unconscious by Craig – he predicted he would hit her 'savagely, viciously' earlier during the link sequence after Sally's story. In the blink of an eye Craig is transported to the audience tables at the Chez Beulah night club and finds himself sitting across from Sylvester Kee and Hugo the dummy. 'My, my, Hugo, we've never played to a murderer before, have we?' asks Kee, prompting Craig to dart for the centre of the dance floor where he is picked out by a spotlight and quickly surrounded by the members of the night club audience. A series of quick cuts sees Craig lifted off his feet by the audience and carried stage left to the incongruity of a prison cell, not unlike the cell where Frere 'asphyxiated' and mashed Hugo to a pulp in Van Straaten's story. The cell is tended by an all-too-familiar jailer, the hearse driver/bus conductor from

Grainger's story who, with a grin and a wink, declares 'just room for one more inside, sir!' Upon being unceremoniously thrown into the cell, Craig meets his end at the hands of a fully reconstituted and independently articulated Hugo, the 'one *more* inside', and with an exaggerated reverse tracking shot his nightmare of horror shrinks before our eyes.

The dream is over and the architectural certainties of Craig's/our world are restored. Those final cell walls have been replaced by the reassuring four walls of Craig's bedroom back in his London home. The reassertion of normality is cemented by the sight of the dome of St. Paul's Cathedral through the bedroom window. The continuity of the dome had inspired the nation during the Blitz in the dying days of 1940, and on VE Day, the 8th of May 1945, during the making of *Dead of Night*, 30,000 people had flocked to the cathedral to give thanks for the end of hostilities in Europe. Perhaps the perpetual loop of the dome's circumference had infiltrated and inspired Craig's dream, the dream that finds no end. The bedside telephone rings, Eliot Foley requests the pleasure of Craig's company at Pilgrim's Farm for the weekend and off we and Craig go again.

The very short scene in Craig's bedroom, before the return to the start of the dream/ film and the repeat shots of Craig's arrival at Pilgrim's Farm, is worthy of a little scrutiny, not least because, depending on your interpretation of the scene, it represents the only moment of 'reality' in the entire film. Within just ninety seconds it manages to contain several components of the dream that has just been dreamt and is about to be dreamt again. It is slightly reminiscent of the brief scene at the end of *The Wizard of Oz* (Victor Fleming 1939), when Dorothy wakes surrounded by the real people upon whom she based the elaborated characters that she met during her Oz dreamtime. Take, for example, the shot of Craig's wife, played by Renee Gadd, sitting on his bed; it is close to a mirror image of Sally sitting singing her lullaby next to Francis Kent's bed in 'Christmas Party'. When his wife opens the bedroom curtains it is a remarkably similar moment to Joyce the nurse's actions at the curtains and window of Hugh Grainger's hospital room in 'Hearse Driver'. Both windows have very similar radiators below them and the turban-style manner in which Craig's wife's wears her headscarf is an echo of Joyce's nurse's cap. Eliot Foley's disembodied and deliberate spelling of his surname – 'F-O-L-E-Y' – over the telephone looks and sounds a little like the stock-in ventriloquial trick of reciting the alphabet while drinking a glass of water. When Craig rises from his bed you'll even find an antique mirror hanging on the bedroom wall behind him.

Once risen, Craig elects to toss a coin in order to decide whether or not he should accept the Pilgrim's Farm reconstruction job and spend a weekend in the country. 'Heads, I go' – the decision is taken. We may wish to ponder that, if Craig's bedroom scene is truly a moment of awakened reality, perhaps one time, maybe next time, the coin will come down tails, the journey to Pilgrim's Farm will not take place and the dream will finally be broken. If on the other hand we choose to regard Craig's apparent waking as false and therefore still a part of his continuing unending dream, we must expect the coin to come down heads every time. Whichever it is, we are seconds away from witnessing the lap dissolve that signals the point at which Craig's seemingly perpetual circuit begins again. After calling heads and deciding to spend a weekend in the country he lights a cigarette; 'It'll help you get rid of those horrible nightmares' says his wife of the invitation, and behind the curls of cigarette smoke Craig's face displays the first signs of unease that we will see once more when he pulls up outside Pilgrim's Farm. The smoking shot is slowed optically and is a little blurred thanks to the dissolve compositing process. Just to accentuate the point at which the end and the beginning of Craig's dream are spliced together the peal of the twelve bells of St. Paul's strikes up and blends into a concluding musical flourish accompanying the end credits laid over the repeating Pilgrim's Farm approach footage. The auditory bridge of that 'Oranges and Lemons' knell from St. Paul's is the cue for Craig the unreliable architect to reacquaint himself with the tour around his personal dream rotunda, an imprisoning structure that he has designed and built, within which exits and entrances are interchangeable and escape forever hinges on the toss of a coin.

'JUST ROOM FOR ONE INSIDE, SIR'

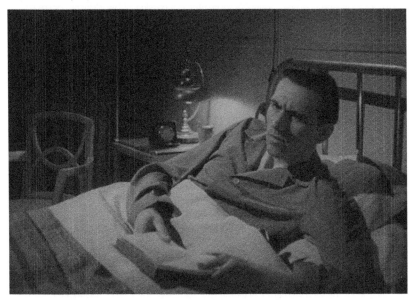

'Quarter to ten. Long past your bedtime.'

'To realise that all your life — you know, all your hate, all your memory, all your pain – it was all the same thing. It was all the same dream. A dream that you had inside a locked room. A dream about being a person. And like a lot of dreams there's a monster at the end of it.' (Detective Rust Cohle [Matthew McConaughey], *True Detective: The Locked Room* [#1.3] HBO 2014)

Whereas 'Linking Narrative' bore a passing resemblance to E.F. Benson's 'The Room in the Tower', 'Hearse Driver', the first and shortest of *Dead of Night*'s nested stories, is very closely based on another of Benson's supernatural tales, specifically 'The Bus-Conductor', first published in *Pall Mall Magazine* in 1906. The path from Benson's tale of premonition, embodied by a dream-like vision of a Victorian hearse, to Basil Dearden's interpretation for the screen passes through a time at the turn of the century when the stubborn residue of Victorian death culture coincided and collided with the emerging scrutiny of the unconscious with its emphasis on the interpretation of dreams.

The generational pall of mourning that descended upon the nation during the decades of lamentation practiced by Queen Victoria after the passing of her Prince Consort provided a dark breeding ground for the widespread morbid fear of death, in particular the fear of premature burial. The historical evidence points to an obsession bordering on mania. Take, for example, the concept of the Safety Coffin; various similar patents were registered during the late eighteenth century and throughout the nineteenth century but the device attributed to Dr. Johann Gottfried Taberger proved popular with the Victorians. Taberger's Safety Coffin featured a mechanism comprised of a piece of string that threaded up from the resting place of the deceased and through the regulation six feet of earth to ground level where it was attached to a bell, the idea being that if the person buried should happen to regain consciousness they would have access to an alarm system that could instigate their disinterment. In case you're wondering, the origins of the term 'saved by the bell' rest here and not in the boxing ring. There are no records to suggest that mechanisms such as Taberger's invention ever resulted in the unearthing of anyone inadvertently buried alive.

This dread of death combined with the development of psychoanalytic theory at the tail-end of the Victorian era places the macabre and illusory 'Bus-Conductor' at something of a cultural intersection. While Freud's landmark 1900 work 'The Interpretation of Dreams' set down the blueprint for the analysis of our nocturnal narratives, his 1914 article 'Erinnern, Weiderholen und Durcharbeiten' (trans. 'Remembering, Repeating and Working-Through') in which he introduced and first defined the psychological phenomenon of 'repetition compulsion' is especially pertinent to 'Hearse Driver' and by extension to the whole of *Dead of Night*. Freud would go on to develop this notion further in his 1920 essay 'Jenseits des Lustprinzips' (trans. 'Beyond the Pleasure Principle'), in which, when describing the aspects of repetitive behaviour, he noted 'dreams occurring in traumatic neuroses have the characteristic of repeatedly bringing the patient back into the situation of his accident' (Freud 1920: 13).

Dashing racer and crash survivor Hugh Grainger's spooky experience is particularly solitary when compared to the later stories in the film. It is centred around an illusory post-traumatic visitation that serves almost as a lap marker along his own life's track, providing fair warning that, having cheated death once by surviving a race accident, an unpleasant fate awaits him at this point on his next circuit of the track. Followers of modern screen horror might wish to reflect upon just how much these same ideas have influenced the various crash survival scenarios and eventual failures to cheat death that run through every single *Final Destination* film.

To return to the source of 'Hearse Driver', a likely precursor to Benson's tale concerns Frederick Hamilton-Temple-Blackwood, 1st Marquess of Dufferin and Ava. A deeply apocryphal story, it tells of an alleged incident dating back to 1879 when Lord Dufferin was on holiday at a friend's manor house in the County Offaly town of Tullamore. Waking at the dead of night he was compelled to look out of his bedroom window whereupon he saw below a man walking across the grounds carrying a coffin on his back. The experience was explained away as nothing more than a bad dream, but years later, during his time as British Ambassador to France, Dufferin found himself in a queue for the elevator in the Grand Hotel in Paris. Just before entering he recognised the elevator attendant as the same man he had seen carrying the coffin in Tullamore, and as a result stepped back and let the elevator car leave without him. It duly plummeted to the bottom of the shaft killing all inside.

It has become clear that Dufferin himself told and retold the anecdote during his lifetime with evermore embroidered elaboration, and that over time, after his death in 1902, it has become a fairly widely circulated urban myth. Its most recognised first print manifestation came in 1921, in the form of a letter attributed to a French psychologist, Monsieur R. de Maratray, and published in Camille Flammarion's book *Death and its Mystery*, although recent research suggests that it was first recorded as early as 1892 through an anonymous second hand account published in the pages of the weekly spiritualist paper *Light: A Journal Devoted to the Higher Interests of Humanity: Here and Hereafter*. Benson was not alone in taking the Dufferin tale and weaving it into his fiction. Eleven years before the publication of 'The Bus-Conductor' Robert W. Chambers referenced it in one of the short stories that comprised his totemic 1895 collection of weird tales *The King in Yellow*, known anew to devotees of the HBO series *True Detective*, the first season of which wove its narrative around aspects of Chambers' novel. One of the stories, 'The Yellow Sign', concerning an artist and his model who are menaced by a peculiar gravedigger, clearly draws on Dufferin. It is worth reproducing a passage from that story in order to illustrate the lineage that led up to what finally became 'Hearse Driver' in *Dead of Night*:

"One night last winter I was lying in bed thinking about nothing at all in particular. I had been posing for you and I was tired out, yet it seemed impossible for me to sleep. I heard the bells in the city ring ten, eleven, and midnight. I must have fallen asleep about midnight because I don't remember hearing the bells after that. It seemed to me that I had scarcely closed my eyes when I dreamed that something impelled me to go to the window. I rose, and raising the sash leaned out. Twenty-fifth Street was deserted as far as I could see. I began to be afraid; everything outside seemed so—so black and uncomfortable. Then the sound of wheels in the distance came to my ears, and it seemed to me as though that was what I must wait for. Very slowly the wheels approached, and, finally, I could make out a vehicle moving along the street. It came nearer and nearer, and when it passed beneath my window I saw it was a hearse. Then, as I trembled with fear, the driver turned and looked straight at me. When I awoke I was standing by the open window shivering with cold, but the black-plumed hearse and the driver were gone. I dreamed this dream again in March last, and again awoke beside the open window. Last night the dream came again. You remember how it was raining; when I awoke, standing at the open window, my night-dress was soaked."

"But where did I come into the dream?" I asked.

"You—you were in the coffin; but you were not dead."

"In the coffin?"

"Yes."

"How did you know? Could you see me?"

"No; I only knew you were there." (Chambers 1895: 66)

At little more than six minutes in length, 'Hearse Driver' is the shortest segment of *Dead of Night*, but for all its brevity it serves a crucial purpose. The first nine minutes of the film are occupied with introducing us to Walter Craig, the guests at Pilgrim's Farm and the curious feeling that the house and those assembled in it seem to be provoking in Craig. While his experience is conveyed as rather peculiar the sense is that he has entered a safe environment and is 'amongst friends', Dr. Van Straaten's dismissive rational scepticism notwithstanding. We are being eased into the film, through the introduction of its cast of characters who, save for Craig, are relaxed and welcoming. It is broad daylight, tea is poured, cigarettes are lit, the company is convivial, on the evidence presented to us we are still in the relatively secure world of the real despite Craig's lurking unease. 'Hearse Driver' puts a stop to that comfortable reality and sets the tone for the frightening moments that will come in the following stories. Put simply, it provides viewers with their first real 'goose bump moment'.

The teller of the tale, Hugh Grainger, seems very happy to kick off the attempts to refute the rationalist assertions of Van Straaten and corroborate Craig's feelings of *déjà vu* with a recollection designed to challenge the psychiatrist's certainty. Addressing Van Straaten he cheerfully counters 'When it comes to seeing the future, something once happened to me that knocks your theories into a cocked hat. Something I'll not forget to my dying day. As a matter of fact it very nearly was my dying day.' In some respects Grainger's story is a souped up and compressed version of Craig's. Both stories begin with the protagonist at the wheel of a vehicle, in Grainger's case driving his racing car at the moment of impact that results in his hospitalisation. Like Craig, Grainger finds himself dazed and confused in a room within which he experiences unexplainable phenomena that echoes the past and predicts the future. The difference between the two is that Grainger's fate is not inexorable; thanks to the curious premonition he is able to act decisively and intervene in the apparently predestined events that would otherwise result in his death. It seems reasonable to consider that, aside from attempting to back up Craig's belief that something very odd is happening to him, Grainger is also seeking through the telling of his tale to reassure Craig that the terrible events he predicts for his own future are not inevitable.

Despite beginning with fast-paced footage of the motor racing crash that lands Grainger in hospital, and the rapid telling of his story, 'Hearse Driver' contains the film's first moment of true stillness. There will be more in the subsequent stories, and these are all important elements in the film's scary effectiveness, but the kernel of Grainger's story begins when he settles down in his bed with a good book after Nurse Joyce wishes him goodnight. The soundtrack to a slow, subtle tracking shot that approaches the recumbent Grainger consists of his leafing through the pages of the book, a song playing on the radio in a room beyond and the quiet ticking of his bedside clock. The ticking alone indicates that time is passing as it should – Joyce informs Grainger that the time is a quarter to ten, 'long past your bedtime', before leaving the room – but when the music stops abruptly mid-song Grainger glances at his clock. The ticking has ceased and the stopped clock now reads a quarter past four.

Placing Grainger in bed at night also deposits the audience in the one place they will already associate with their own nightmares. In a film that is all about a recurring bad dream it comes as no surprise to find the vehicle of our nightmares, the bed, featuring repeatedly throughout. From the outset we learn from Foley's greeting that Craig has been hired to extend Pilgrim's Farm by 'at least two more bedrooms'. After Grainger's story centred around his hospital bed we see a succession of beds in the following stories; Sally puts the ghostly Francis Kent to bed and sings him a lullaby in her story; the mirror in Joan's story is fixed to the walls of the bedrooms in both old and new apartments with the ornate four-poster a constant presence in 'the other room'; the golfing story culminates in a scene involving the wedding night bed; and the ventriloquist's dummy story includes several different beds, those in Frere's and Kee's hotel rooms, the prison cell bed where Frere has his final conversation with Hugo the dummy and the sanatorium bed where Frere lies possessed of Hugo's voice and personality. Not forgetting the bed at home in London where we see Craig 'wake' from his dream at the film's end.

The bed, our stationary carriage of birth, sex, dreams, sickness and death in which we sleep off a third of our lives, has long been a primary staple environment for scares throughout supernatural literature and cinema. Horror writers and film-makers have succeeded if their work inspires a fear of the place of sleep among their audience. Cinematic illustrations of bed-bound dreams and nightmares started out in a quite comical vein. Georges Méliès' brief but playful 1896 film *The Nightmare* showed a sleeper beneath his bedroom window haunted by a woman, a pierrot and a minstrel before an amusingly surreal interaction with a full moon. In more recent decades beds have featured in some of the more horrific and frightening scenes in horror cinema. Rosemary Woodhouse (Mia Farrow) drifts off into a drugged oblivion and is transported on her bed through a series of dreams before being impregnated by Satan in *Rosemary's Baby* (Roman Polanski 1968). The possessed Regan MacNeil (Linda Blair) spends a good deal of time lying in, tethered to or hovering above her bed in *The Exorcist* (William Friedkin 1973). Glen Lantz (Johnny Depp) is eviscerated and reduced to a liquid torrent of gore spouting up from the centre of his bed in *A Nightmare on Elm Street* (Wes Craven 1984). As part of her analysis of the Wes Craven *Elm Street* films in the special issue of *The Luminary* entitled 'Sleep(less) Beds: Awakening, Journey, Movement, Stasis', Katharina Rein suggests that in those films especially 'the bed is turned into a symbol of horror and is established as a possible portal into the world of deadly nightmares...beds constitute [a] central motif [and] function as an entry point to a different reality'. (Rein 2013: 15)

The strange temporal stasis that Grainger experiences is cleverly accentuated by the film's soundtrack; indeed the near-silence that accompanies the stopping of the clock suggests that he/we have entered a vacuum of sorts. Most of us will recall the classroom science experiment that proves the inability of sound to travel in a vacuum, usually taking the form of a ringing bell contained within a glass vessel gradually silenced as the air is pumped out. When the sounds of the ticking clock and the song playing on the radio are sucked out of Grainger's room we become more acutely aware that we have entered a suspended state. The removal of lively music and the introduction of deathly quiet is used twice more elsewhere in the film; the hostess's piano playing in the large open plan ground floor space in 'Christmas Party' shrinks to near-silence when Sally ascends the stairs to the upper reaches of the country house, and in 'Ventriloquist's Dummy' Elizabeth Welch's rendition of the song 'The Hullalooba' on the stage of Chez Beulah dissipates once Sylvester Kee goes backstage and enters Maxwell Frere's dressing room.[8]

This void is subtly signalled when Joyce removes a vase of cut flowers as she bids Grainger goodnight and leaves the room. Her action recalls a belief, still fairly entrenched at the time of the film's making, that flowers in a hospital room are bad for the patient because they suck oxygen out of the air. There's little science to back this up, although it is true that while plants absorb carbon dioxide and emit oxygen during the day, the process changes at night. During the hours of darkness they absorb more oxygen than they produce, and they emit carbon dioxide. In truth however this is very unlikely to have any negative impact on a recovering patient but it was, perhaps still is in some quarters, an old wives' tale that persisted. Perhaps by removing the flowers Joyce, the woman who Grainger will eventually marry, is unconsciously helping him to survive the coming shortage of air in the room. The withdrawal of the vase could also suggest that

Joyce is sparing her husband-to-be the portent of a graveside floral tribute.

Another of Joyce's actions before leaving the room, the drawing of the curtains, is more in tune with those Victorian beliefs concerning the marking of the moment of death, and as such could also be seen as a warning signifier of Grainger's possible fate. Furthermore, when she tells Grainger that it is long past his bedtime she picks up the bedside clock in order to tell him that it is a quarter to ten, and in so doing is the last to touch the clock before it moves to a quarter past four and stops at the beginning of Grainger's bizarre premonition. Another Victorian tradition was to ensure that when a person passed away the clocks in the room in which they died were stopped. Perhaps Joyce's intervention with Grainger's bedside clock is a further unconscious attempt to forewarn of or hold back the spectre of death. Although this collection of signifiers may be incidental and unintended on the part of the film-makers Joyce is conspicuously industrious in her actions before leaving Grainger in the room alone, suggesting a pattern of pre-warnings, and given that we will learn later of the subsequent marriage to her patient, it is tempting to regard Joyce the nurse as fulfilling a white-clad protective guardian angel role in opposition to the black-clad hearse driving harbinger of doom that Grainger will go on to witness below his window.

Grainger's vacuum of stillness remains practically silent from the point when the radio music cuts out and the clock stops ticking up to the pale twittering of birdsong that serenades the incongruous daylight outside of the window and the discordant sting of music courtesy of Georges Auric's score that announces the presence of the hearse. Just about the only audible sound between these points can be detected when Grainger, still in bed, glances across to the drawn curtains at his window. During a six-second shot of the gently fluttering curtains the sound of a passing car can be heard.

In his deeply penetrative and insightful article about *Dead of Night* in a 2010 issue of *The Psychoanalytic Quarterly*, which you will find referred to several times in this book, Leon Balter suggests that the car sound is not simply traffic passing below his window. Indeed when Grainger opens the curtains (and presupposing that the entirety of his view from the window – grounds, buildings and all – is not a vision) we will see that his room looks out onto the quiet internal courtyard of the nursing home rather than the road outside the front of the building. Balter infers that the sound of the passing motor vehicle relates back to the crash that put Grainger in hospital, and links into the guilt that he is suffering, expressed as delirious ramblings in the story's initial post-crash hospital scene, provoked by the concern that he may have been responsible for the death of another driver involved in the crash (Balter 2010). On this basis Grainger is haunted by the worry that he has cheated death possibly at the expense of another. All of which taps in neatly to Freud's ideas of trauma and guilt associated with that notion of 'repetition compulsion'. Dr. Albury (Robert Wyndham), Grainger's treating physician at the clinic, explains the vision to his recovering patient in relative layman's terms – 'that apparition of death was what we call the psychological crisis' – to reassure Grainger that he isn't 'going crackers'. Albury's attempt to reassure Grainger with a dash of common sense does indeed help the convalescence process, but when Grainger subsequently leaves Albury's care and approaches the double-decker bus that pulls up to the stop outside the nursing home, collecting passengers at his quarter past four 'time of death', he comes face to face with the bus conductor who is the spitting image of the hearse driver from his vision and capitulates to his sixth sense feeling that it would not be wise to board the bus.

'That hearse driver was sent to me as a warning.'

Which brings us to the phrase that dominates Grainger's story; after struggling to process the unexpected switch from the darkness of 9.45pm to the sunlit brightness of 4.15pm that greets his gaze out of the window during his hospital room premonition, Grainger glances down to behold a Victorian black horse-drawn hearse, the driver of which cranes his neck to make eye contact and exclaims 'Just room for one inside, sir', with a jerk of his head to indicate that he is talking about the empty carriage behind him. We will hear this exact same line again spoken by the look-alike bus conductor at the end of Grainger's story, and once again with a small but important variation at the bitter end of Walter Craig's nightmare. Regarding this phrase, Leon Balter makes another interesting observation in his *Psychoanalytic Quarterly* article by suggesting that in one form or another it echoes through every subsequent story in the film. In 'Christmas Party' there is arguably only room for one person in the alcove hiding place that Sally finds during the game of Sardines. In 'Haunted Mirror' Peter only sees himself reflected in the room in the mirror, there is seemingly no room for his wife Joan even when they both stand in front of it. In 'Golfing Story' there is only room for one man in the relationship that George Parratt has formed with his new bride Mary (Peggy Bryan), in fact by striving to exclude his golfing partner Larry Potter from the liaison the phrase could be construed to take on a more overtly sexual aspect. The same can be said of 'Ventriloquist's Dummy'; there is only room for one ventriloquist's hand pulling the strings inside Hugo but in the bizarre love triangle between Frere, Kee and the dummy the proprietary rights of access to Hugo's innards may extend beyond hands.

The phrase rebounds around Grainger's story; it is more than just the verbal augury heard during his vision that will find a matching echo in the words of the bus conductor when Grainger leaves hospital, thereby enabling him to take a step back from the bus and cheat death a second time. There is also just room for him inside first racing car, then hospital bed before he is witness to the vision of his potential fate, alone inside a coffin. His capsule story is his carriage within which, through the advent of a fateful vision that he cannot pass off as a purely neurological aberration, he is able to intervene and draw back from his apparently predestined demise.

Along with serving as a compression of Craig's narrative and a first container of the film's recurrent tropes, 'Hearse Driver' is a distilled reverberation of the fear of conscious disbelief, a fear that is not only at the heart of every element of the film but also in the hearts and minds of its intended audience. Grainger appears to experience a waking dream, he is not shown closing his eyes and lapsing into sleep before he 'sees' the hearse. Instead he is sitting up in bed reading when his experience begins. So he is convinced that his experience is real, however frighteningly unbelievable. 'It couldn't have been a dream, I hadn't had time to fall asleep', he explains to Dr. Albury subsequently. Only upon returning to his bed after seeing the hearse does he put his hands up to his head in an effort to 'wake up' and make sense of what he has just witnessed. At the very end of his story, as he watches the double-decker bus crash off the side of the bridge, Grainger closes his eyes in an effort to deny the appalling reality, and as he lowers his head the brim of his hat acts almost as an eyelid, lowering over our view of his face in a masterful dissolve back to the scene at Pilgrim's Farm.

We find instances of the closing, covering, rubbing and repeated blinking of eyes, usually as an attempt to determine reality from dream, deposited throughout the film. Craig's first sight of Pilgrim's Farm elicits a quizzical blink, and is followed moments later by an exaggerated opening and closing of his eyelids in a very evident effort to clear his head once inside the house – 'So it isn't a dream this time.' Sally is 'it' in a game of Blind Man's Buff at the opening of her story and has her eyes covered by a blindfold. She will blink hard and bury her face into the comforting embrace of Jimmy Watson's mother when she realises that she has just encountered a ghost. Jimmy's eyes are covered at the beginning of the game of Sardines, as are the eyes of all of the partygoers when Craig attempts to hide during his final nightmare. In the early stages of his interaction with the mirror Peter keeps closing and reopening his eyes in the hope that the other room will have disappeared and been replaced by the familiarity of his own bedroom. Larry Potter's ghost hides his eyes from George Parratt's wedding night smooch with new wife Mary. The movements of Hugo the dummy's eyelids suggest malevolent life blinking into being, especially at the point of his appearance in Craig's final nightmare. His glasses broken, Van Straaten sends Grainger off to find his spare pair – 'I'm lost without them' – as he accepts Craig's dream towards the end of the film, sitting down to listen to and psychoanalyse the dreamer while rubbing his tired eyes in the process.

Dead of Night is a film about false waking, or perhaps more accurately the struggle to 'come round'. Taken as an indicator of the national state of mind, British cinema audiences in 1945 were just rubbing their eyes and beginning to recover a collective consciousness in the weeks and months after the cessation of war, seeking as they were to wake up from and move beyond the living nightmare of the last six years. Grainger's head injury and subsequent strange episode in 'Hearse Driver' taps into this shared desire for revival beyond survival.

There are several similarities between Grainger's experiences and those of Squadron Leader Peter Carter (David Niven) in Michael Powell and Emeric Pressburger's *A Matter of Life and Death* (1946), released a little over a year after *Dead of Night*. Both Grainger and Carter appear to suffer variations on survivor guilt. Carter himself is at a loss to explain his apparent escape from the clutches of certain death after jumping from his stricken plane without a parachute. Dr. Frank Reeves (Roger Livesey) takes a neurological line not unlike Dr. Albury in 'Hearse Driver' and puts Carter's seizures down to an earlier concussion affecting the temporal lobe. When a seizure takes hold time appears to stand still around Carter; he observes Dr. Reeves and June (Kim Hunter) frozen midway through a game of table tennis and later, as June looks on anxiously outside the operating theatre where Carter is about to undergo surgery, his out-of-body experience leads him away from the static surgical team and past June who is now rooted to the spot. Just before he leaps up from the operating table, as the anaesthetic takes effect prior to his brain surgery, we are privy to Carter's point of view and look on as a giant eyelid, not unlike the brim of Grainger's hat in 'Hearse Driver', eclipses his/our view of the operating theatre ceiling. Carter survives the surgery, and upon coming round from the anaesthetic in the film's final scene, with his head bandaged much as Grainger's is when he is first admitted to hospital after his motor racing crash, a nurse can be seen opening the hospital room curtains to let in daylight.

It's interesting to compare this shot of the nurse opening the curtains to the very similar shot of Joyce the nurse *closing* the curtains in Grainger's hospital room. *A Matter of Life and Death*, after its journey through the frequently dark and uncertain terrain between life and death, looks out ultimately on to the broad, sunlit uplands promised in Churchill's speech in 1940 anticipating the Battle of Britain. *Dead of Night* by comparison was still feeling its way in the dark and doing battle with fear and guilt, with defeat of these two enemies and the locating of a path to a brighter future absolutely not guaranteed. John Orr, in his 2010 book *Romantics and Modernists in British Cinema,* succinctly compares the two films, declaring them to be:

like day and night: one is in breathtaking Technicolor and deals in metaphysical healing, while the other is in black and white and deals in perpetual nightmare...When your country has been battered by a monstrous war, you want to savour victory and then move on. That is what *A Matter of Life and Death* explicitly allows, and what *Dead of Night* implicitly denies. (Orr 2010: 89)

Once Grainger has lowered the 'eyelid' brim of his hat and we dissolve back to the drawing room at Pilgrim's Farm it's clear that the racing driver is unwilling to believe that his vision was anything less than a warning. Sally wonders why the other passengers on the bus apparently failed to receive or heed similar warnings, which prompts Mrs. Foley, Eliot's mother, to suggest that they were perhaps 'doubting Thomases' like Dr. Van Straaten. We might expand upon Sally's thought and question why, possessed of the knowledge that the bus will crash, Grainger didn't do the decent thing and alert the passengers that if they were to stay on board they would surely die. Perhaps by saving himself alone we are afforded a final illustration that within the confines of his warning, there really is only room for one inside.

'Just room for one inside, sir.'

'I'M NOT FRIGHTENED...I'M NOT FRIGHTENED...'

> Whenever five or six English-speaking people meet around a fire on Christmas Eve,
> they start telling each other ghost stories. Nothing satisfies us on Christmas Eve but
> to hear each other tell authentic anecdotes about spectres. It is a genial, festive season,
> and we love to muse upon graves, and dead bodies, and murders and blood.
> (Jerome K. Jerome: *Told After Supper*. London, The Leadenhall Press, 1891)

Scripted by Ealing stalwart Angus MacPhail and directed by Cavalcanti, 'Christmas Party'
is the only *Dead of Night* story to be based on actual recorded events, specifically the
Constance Kent case of 1865 which saw the teenage Constance convicted, wrongly
in many minds, of the murder of her half-brother Francis five years earlier at the Kent
family home in the Somerset village of Road.[9] The case caused much press excitement
and public gossip in its day and was reawakened by the Kate Summerscale book *The
Suspicions of Mr Whicher or The Murder at Road Hill House* published by Bloomsbury in
2009, later dramatised for television. Despite not naming the country house setting of
her tale Sally O'Hara, played by the then-fifteen-year-old Sally Ann Howes, locates it
accurately in her introduction – 'We were spending Christmas down in Somerset' – and
the murder case is explicitly referred to during the story.[10] While the case has no direct
association with Christmas the blood-curdling nature of the crime lends itself nicely to
the festive tradition of frequently gruesome fireside storytelling.

The association of Christmas in the shared English cultural memory with the telling,
as well as the setting, of ghost stories is a relatively modern development. Much like
our present day concept of Christmas, this spinning of ghostly yuletide yarns is largely
an invention of the Victorian era, though the roots of wintertime ghost stories do go
back much further. That Jerome K. Jerome was able to poke fun at it in the introduction
to his short story collection *Told After Supper* is an indication as to how prevalent the
phenomenon had become by its publication in 1891. M.R. James concocted his famously
chilling tales to entertain friends and students over Christmas Eve fireside gatherings in
his rooms at Kings College, Cambridge. Henry James' 1898 novella *The Turn of the Screw*,
about a house disturbed by restless malevolent spirits haunting the young children who
live there begins as a tale told at Christmas to assembled guests in a country residence.

As discussed earlier, the author most commonly associated with ghostly tales for the Christmas period, and for much of our shared cultural conception of the Victorian era, is Charles Dickens. His most famous ghost story, *A Christmas Carol*, contains a variety of hauntings and ghostly visions of past, present and future. The encounters in these tales bear some resemblance to Sally's own experience which is less the vision of a ghostly apparition than a transportation to another time and place, much like Scrooge's encounters in the book. Unlike Scrooge, however, Sally can interact with the ghost of the young Francis Kent. Whilst Dickens' famous Christmas tale is ultimately comforting and has been increasingly sentimentalised through its various screen adaptations, it is worth noting that the idea of the death of a child is central to the effectiveness of the story. Also noteworthy is that Dickens followed the story of the murder of Francis Kent closely, indeed was one of the more vocal doubters of Constance Kent's guilt at the time of her trial, and based the character of Sergeant Cuff in his final unfinished novel *The Mystery of Edwin Drood* on Jack Whicher, the chief investigating officer on the Kent case. Wilkie Collins also utilised parts of the case in his 1868 novel *The Moonstone*.

The nineteenth-century winters described by Dickens and his contemporaries have given us much of the common iconography of Christmas time, particularly of deep snow and long bitterly cold evenings. There is a striking meteorological connection between Dickens and a famous house party that took place in 1816 at the Villa Diodati, a mansion by the shores of Lake Geneva, alluded to by Roger Clarke in his book *A Natural History of Ghosts* (2012). The gathering at the villa took place in the 'year without summer' brought about by the eruption of Mount Tambora in the East Indies the previous year. Those assembled at the villa included Mary Shelley and Dr. John William Polidori who joined the other guests in retreating from the foul weather brought on by the atmospheric change and told each other ghost stories to pass the time. As a consequence Shelley and Polidori went on to write *Frankenstein* and *The Vampyr* respectively. The climatic trauma which caused their enforced seclusion and provided the spark for an explosion in Gothic fiction was also to trigger the decades-long series of cold winters which Dickens and other Victorian writers were to so memorably describe in their own fictions.

A haunted house and childhood games; burgeoning adolescence and ghostly activity; Christmas fires and tales of uncanny happenings. All these serve to make 'Christmas

Party' the most notionally traditional of the tales presented in the film. Sally, the youngest of the guests at Pilgrim Farm, is an adolescent girl full of excitement at the arrival of Walter Craig with his fascinating claims of *déjà vu*. She is eager to join the adults in their drawing room conversations, but is still possessed of a childlike enthusiasm and attendant lack of tact. The story is from a time before the idea of the teenager as a modern entity existed with any significant cultural weight of its own. It was an uncomfortable time of transition when adult clothing was worn awkwardly and a youthful yearning to be taken seriously whilst being patronised by grown-ups awaited the phenomenon of youth culture that would explode a decade later. Gauche and inexperienced though she might appear in the farmhouse with the worldly adults, Sally is nonetheless coming into maturity and her experiences at the Christmas party are significant in that light. *Dead of Night* was remarkably anticipatory of several future film tropes, and one might venture to consider 'Christmas Party' as a contender for the first example of 'teen horror', the sub-genre that would emerge in the cinema of subsequent decades once the spending power and marketing potential of the new 'teenager' culture had been realised. A stretch perhaps, but we know that teen horror cinema is routinely defined by its themes of sexual maturation and rite of passage, so we can say that the subtext of Sally's story is consistent with this.

Sally's emerging sexual maturity is presented through her confident and untroubled rejection of the advances of the more sexually immature character of Jimmy Watson who, as the only adolescent male party guest of comparable age, displays a keen interest in Sally. We first see her at the party, playing 'it' in a game of blind man's buff where she teasingly identifies Jimmy through his 'silly nose': a phallic analogue emphasised by the much more prominent and erect nose on the mask which he has pushed back from his face. While most of the other children at the party are wearing more typically childish fancy dress costumes, Jimmy wears the costume of Harlequin and Sally's resembles that of Columbina, the love interest of Harlequin from the Italian tradition of *Commedia dell'arte*. The character of Columbina is traditionally the most sensible of the supporting cast of characters whilst capable of flirtation and impertinence, in keeping with Sally's burgeoning maturity and sexual confidence. This is in contrast with Jimmy's more playful but overbearing and attention-seeking behaviour. The costumes have a more adult and sexualised interpretation than the childish costumes worn by the other party guests.

Despite the role of Columbina as Harlequin's mistress, Jimmy is doomed to remain unrequited in his advances to Sally, his childish enthusiasm for party games placing him on the wrong side of Sally's incipient adulthood. Jimmy teases her with the graphic details of the murder of Francis Kent, informing her that it took place in the house some eighty years earlier. This attempt to impress Sally with his access to dark secrets does not have the desired effect, and his first awkward attempt at physical intimacy is effortlessly brushed aside. However, she willingly takes his hand when he promises to show her a better hiding place up the spiral staircase to the attic. She also flirts with him by engaging in the acting out of ghostly manifestation in the dusty attic, including a playful scream, but roundly rejects his clumsy attempt to kiss her. Jimmy's pantomime of a haunting is all effect and cliché, whereas Sally speculates as to the guilt of a haunting spirit, her more mature empathetic outlook again contrasting with Jimmy's limited emotional development.

'Believe it or not, this house is haunted.'

After having his advances in the attic rejected by Sally, who pulls a dusty rag over his head causing him to sneeze, Jimmy assumes Sally has gone to join the rest of the children at the party and runs downstairs to rejoin the world of childish games. Poor

Jimmy's uncontrolled sneeze is an involuntary loss of physical control common to teenage boys upon first physical encounter with a girl in somewhat more intimate situations. Sally ignores the exit of her disappointing suitor and remains in the dark attic with its shadowy forms and faded memories, exploring, opening doors long closed and forgotten. The attic is a place of darker knowledge and hidden meaning with secrets to be unlocked. The door at the back of the attic room leads her to a decrepit and dingy corridor, apparently long abandoned. As a party guest and a stranger to the house, the attic reaches are literally as well as metaphorically unexplored territory for Sally, but she proceeds with no great sense of foreboding, instead she remains curious to explore and is not inordinately alarmed or surprised to find herself in a well-decorated nursery room at the end of the corridor or by the sound of a weeping child which leads her to it. The game of Sardines, and with it the realm of childish pastimes, is forgotten when she comes upon the little boy in obvious distress. It is an encounter which requires a more mature aspect of Sally to come to the fore.

Her interaction with Francis assumes a sisterly, even maternal tone from the outset; Francis observes that his own sister Constance, Sally's dark alter ego, is the same age as Sally, 'grown up' as he puts it. Sally responds with a hint of regret, that the other girls at the party seem 'much younger' than her, as if noticing this for the first time and recognising her own growing distance from childhood. She asks Francis if he will accompany her to join the rest of the children downstairs where it is warmer; although Francis' bedroom is clean and well decorated, there is no fire in the hearth; there might be the suggestion of embers, but they do not crackle or glow, suggesting a place frozen in time. Sally is focussed on comforting the child and she assumes an adult role, singing Francis a lullaby, adapting to this motherly aspect of herself with ease. In keeping with the other female roles in the film, her strength is called upon in aid of a damaged male psyche and given unquestioningly, though unlike Joan Cortland in 'Haunted Mirror' there is no sense in which she can actually save Francis. More chilling for the audience, in light of what is to be revealed to Sally, is the realisation that she is actually leaving him to his fate at the hands of his sister.

On taking her leave of the now calmed and comforted Francis tucked up in his bed, she does not register his 'goodbye' in response to her 'goodnight' and is greeted as soon as she opens the door by the cries of the children who are beckoning her back to the realm of childish concerns. Welcomed back to the group, she explains where she has been, and ignores Jimmy's impotent demands for her attention. Sally might not yet be aware of what she has experienced, but she has no need of Jimmy and what he thinks he knows. Upon rejoining the party in the brightly lit spaces downstairs, Sally walks through the excited throng of children and discusses her experience with her hostess Mrs. Watson, their relatively serious and adult conversation at odds with the boisterousness of the crowd of children at the party.

As the closing scene of the sequence, Sally's reaction to the knowledge that the child she had encountered was the ghost of the dead Francis Kent can be viewed as a slight mis-step. The delivery of the lines 'I'm not frightened…I'm not frightened…' before collapsing into Mrs. Watson's arms begging to be comforted seems awkward and Sally Ann Howes' delivery somewhat uncertain and stilted. However the context here is important. Sally has passed a threshold through which she cannot return: her encounter with Francis is a loss of innocence, a journey which she undertook willingly up and through the dark places at the top of the house. On hearing the deeply unsettling news of the nature of her encounter, she attempts a retreat into a place where an adult touch will comfort her in the way she comforted the dead Francis. Unfortunately for Sally this is not possible; she seeks the comfort due a child when presented with horrors real or imagined, but for her it is too late for this kind of consolation. She is an adult now, marked by darker experiences of life which cannot be unlearned, forced by these experiences to grow up quickly as so many children were during the war years.

Sally's journey from cheery playfulness to dark seriousness via a traumatic, innocence-depriving threshold is entirely in keeping with Brazilian director Cavalcanti's outsider view of the British during and after the Second World War. In his BBC blog discussion of the pantomime of British national character since the war, the journalist Adam Curtis makes extensive use of *Dead of Night* and the approach taken by its makers to illustrate his point. He contends that:

> Cavalcanti thought that the British had a dangerously false vision of themselves – a twee artifice of forced jollity… for Cavalcanti and many of his generation who experienced the Second World War, post-war Britain was possessed by a false and shallow cheerfulness. (Curtis 2012)

'Whistling winds…clanking chains…bloodcurdling screams…'

This view of the national psyche was especially in evidence in Cavalcanti's 1942 film *Went the Day Well?*, a propaganda feature that managed to double as a darkly transgressive piece, and one that in its latter stages also featured a country house full of children who are forced ahead of time to come to terms with the harsh grown up realities of life during wartime. After 'Golfing Story', 'Christmas Party' has tended to be the *Dead of Night* story least admired by critics, but taken as an adjunct to Cavalcanti's dissection of strangulated Britishness found in *Went the Day Well?* it is a potent vignette worthy of merit. By fashioning Sally and Jimmy as Columbina and Harlequin the director introduced the foreign origin and pushed it through the quintessentials of the traditional English Christmas ghost story, via a passage of adolescent awakening, in an attempt to prise open that part of the British character he considered to be ordinarily brushed under the carpet and suppressed.

The little pantomime of ghostly rattles and screams which Jimmy and Sally enact in invoking the concept of a stereotypical haunting is very different from Sally's actual encounter with the ghost of Francis Kent. In his taxonomy of hauntings and ghostly manifestations, all of which have been richly mined in literature and cinema, Roger Clarke categorises the experience Sally has in the nursery room as a time-slip. The nature of time-slip haunting is that rather than an encounter with a restless or vengeful soul, the person who experiences the haunting finds him or herself stepping into an environment seemingly from an earlier era, where they see people from that time going about their business, either interacting with the visitor or seemingly oblivious to their presence. In reported claims of time-slip encounters some kind of liminal space is crossed into the environment, and in Sally's case it is the corridor from the attic to Francis Kent's bedroom. The idea of a time-slip ghost story had already been used by Ealing in *The Halfway House*, directed by Basil Dearden and an un-credited Cavalcanti, and scripted by 'Christmas Party' writer Angus McPhail. The house itself in *The Halfway House* may be a phantom but is preserved in time and the travellers interact freely with their hosts unaware of the subtle clues around them, being so wrapped up in their own lives and past mistakes. *The Halfway House* is not a horror story, but its influence on *Dead of Night* in shaping the type of encounter experienced by Sally is palpable.

The decrepit state of the corridor and the dusty neglected air of the attic room do not suggest that a perfectly preserved and decorated bedroom is likely to be found off the corridor, or that this part of the house is even accessed regularly. Jimmy has already told us that no one has witnessed any ghostly activity in the house in the six months they have been there, which raises the question of why it is Sally who encounters the dead child while other members of the household have not. In terms of the story, there is no real reason for this – nor need there be – but in horror fiction the connection between female sexuality and the supernatural is well explored, particularly in the setting of the 'Old Dark House'.

The discussion in the earlier chapter looking at 'Linking Narrative' considered numerous aspects of architecture and how this relates to the inducement of fear in *Dead of Night*, but the Watson residence in 'Christmas Party' is the most extensively explored building in the film and therefore should come closest to conforming to the 'Old Dark House' convention, on paper at least. The 'Old Dark House' is a long-standing staple setting of horror literature and cinema, and a cornerstone of Gothic literature in general, surviving lapses into parody to provide rich material and an enduring and surprisingly malleable stage for horrific encounters and ghostly tales. From the early days of Gothic literature, a particular strand of horror romanticism has depended on the inhabitants, properties and atmosphere of the 'Old Dark House'. John C. Tibbets points this out in his contribution to *British Horror Cinema* (2002), placing the origin of this idea on the battlements of Elsinore where the ghost of Hamlet's father haunts a royal house torn by fratricide and incest. That the dwelling must be troubled, and bear an inheritance of trauma is an essential element of the 'Old Dark House' as a literary and cinematic trope.

'Christmas Party' contains some of Michael Relph's most ambitious set designs for the film, allowing Cavalcanti room to move his camera and frame characters in very different ways to the methods he would employ in 'Ventriloquist's Dummy', his second *Dead of Night* contribution. In that story confined spaces, directional expressionist lighting and static composition are employed deliberately to create a sense of claustrophobia, reinforcing the idea of the struggle for the occupation of Maxwell Frere's mind. 'Christmas Party' by contrast has the most open interior setting in all the stories, at least at the outset when the party is in full swing. Cavalcanti takes advantage of the space and grandeur for the initial impression, one that initially plays against the 'Old Dark House' convention. Here is an open world of childhood games which Cavalcanti shoots in a style more akin to his preferred poetic realism, framing the action naturalistically and fluidly, only becoming more tightly framed when the action narrows to Sally and Jimmy and their journey from the curtained alcove where Sally first hides during the game of Sardines to the narrow spiral staircase up to the attic. Even here, and in the dingy corridor to Francis' room, there is no attempt to force the conventions of 'Old Dark House' stories; the attic and the corridor are not sinister but old and hidden or forgotten places for Sally to explore, licensed by her new maturity to leave behind the comforting, crowded bustle of childhood.

The Innocents, Jack Clayton's acclaimed screen version of *The Turn of the Screw* from 1961, fully explored the theme of childhood innocence versus perverted adult sexuality, making full use of the 'Old Dark House' setting. Two years later *The Haunting* (Robert Wise 1963) set the benchmark for subtle horror in a haunted house, with the building itself becoming a character and instrument of terror in its own right. 'Christmas Party' sits a little awkwardly in such company as by and large it eschews the conventions these later films built and improved upon. The overall effect of Sally's journey up through the house and into Francis Kent's bedroom is strangely comforting; it isn't really played for scares; what we have at most is a sense of unease, certainly the juxtaposition of stumbling upon the bedroom is less startling and contradictory compared to the daylight view from Hugh Grainger's hospital window in the preceding 'Hearse Driver'. The story's real scare is delivered at its end, when Sally becomes aware of what has just happened to her. In the rush of her new-found maturity she struggles to process the shock and unsettling sadness that comes with contemplating the violent death of a child. Not only that, Sally's upset is heightened by the thought that her care and attention for Francis was, and will always be, unsuccessful in preventing his violent death.

And herein lies the potency of that pay-off for the audiences of 1945. The use of the ghost of a child as the central aspect of 'Christmas Party' highlights one of the anxieties of Second World War Britain; the trauma and danger presented by aerial bombing and long-range rockets placed the country's children in peril from a war whose battle lines were hundreds of miles away. Thousands of children were evacuated to the country from big cities to escape the devastation wrought by the long-distance Nazi onslaught. The party in which we meet Sally is populated by many children but there are only two adults present and we only hear one speak: Mrs Watson the hostess. We do see an elderly man in the background in what appears to be the garb of a butler, but the majority of the revellers are young children with a handful of older adolescents. This absence of adults of parenting age is striking; the older adolescents are seen to assume a shepherding role in much the same way that many young people were forced to on the home front through the absence of parents either fighting the war or working to keep the nation going. Children raised by children, already a fact among the working poor, became more prevalent during the war, and the maturity in girls of Sally's age came to be called upon early. The responsibility of protecting younger siblings from harm was a heavy burden for many older children still of school age and the dread of failure to prevent their death must have played on many adolescent minds.

After the conclusion to Sally's story, back at Pilgrim's Farm, Van Straaten is at his most dismissive; as Leon Balter explains in his article, the psychiatrist sees it as a 'hysterical dissociative episode with hallucinatory features' (op. cit.: 766). Van Straaten makes reference to Saint Teresa of Avila, whose religious visions were reportedly of an erotic nature. Saint Teresa was the subject of the only film – Nigel Wingrove's *Visions of*

'Stay with me. It's better now you've come.'

Ecstasy from 1989 – ever to have been banned by the BBFC on the grounds of
blasphemy. The mix of female sexuality and religion proved as problematic for the
censor as it has been for the Church where it was so often punished and feared. Horror
cinema, by comparison, has mined this sexuality both progressively and regressively but
has always admitted its power. Balter takes time to expand on Van Straaten's theory
in elaborate Freudian terms, which also go some way to contextualising the long
association between horror and sex. It resolves, in the manifestation of Francis Kent,
to the creation of an imaginary younger brother figure in Sally's mind onto which she
projects her own pre-adolescent masculinity. The hallucination, as Balter terms it, comes
after Sally has been sexually stimulated in a way she is not yet ready to accept. The
fantasy of partial decapitation, presented by the knowledge of Francis Kent's demise,
is an eradication of her boyishness so as to advance her burgeoning sexuality. It is also
a symbolic castration, in keeping with the overall theme of male sexual anxiety in the
rest of the film. Slasher films from the 1970s and 1980s were notorious to the point of

parody for punishing the sexually confident female by making her the victim of whatever masked killer stalked the movie, often early in the story. This trope reflected a perversely prurient conservatism inconsistent with the subject matter. The connection between female sexuality and horror was better explored in films like *Repulsion* (Roman Polanski 1965), in which a sexually troubled young woman (Catherine Deneuve) is driven mad when left alone in a London flat, and *Carrie* (Brian de Palma 1976) where repressed sexuality collides with a teenage girl's adolescence to memorable effect.

Whatever the merits of Balter's dissection of Sally's story, the feel of the piece is subtly disturbing, rather than horrific, in service of the slowly mounting sense of dread the film as a whole requires. Its effectiveness stems more from the reflection on what Sally's encounter was, not from the encounter itself, or the setting. It is the realisation that little Francis Kent still awaits his awful fate in the time-slip reality he inhabits, and that Sally would be incapable of preventing it even if she had understood more at the time of her encounter – this terrible event will always happen. It foreshadows and complements the larger idea of the dream from which Walter Craig cannot awaken with the idea of a fate that cannot be escaped. With its notions of an unseen murderous presence and a dark mirror-image alter ego in the absent form of Constance Kent, it sets the stage for the chillingly memorable story which is to follow.

'SOMETHING EVIL, MONSTROUSLY EVIL'

Strange, that there are dreams, that there are mirrors.

Strange that the ordinary, worn-out ways

Of every day encompass the imagined

And endless universe woven by reflections.

(Jorge Luis Borges, 'Mirrors', in *Dreamtigers*, Mildred Boyer and Harold Morland, tr.

[1960] Austin: University of Texas Press, 1964)

'Haunted Mirror' is the first of *Dead of Night*'s two segments based on an original story by John V. Baines. Baines shared the film's screenplay credit with Angus MacPhail, and both also received story contributor credits alongside H.G. Wells and E.F. Benson. *Dead of Night* marked Baines' first screen credit, and also provided Robert Hamer with his first formal credit as a director. Hamer had joined Ealing in 1940 and edited a couple of the studio's wartime propaganda pieces – *Ships With Wings* (Sergei Nolbandov 1941) and *The Foreman Went to France* (Charles Frend 1942) – before playing an important part in the writing and completion of the docudrama *San Demetrio London* (Charles Frend 1943), a significant release in relation to Balcon's 'realism or tinsel' positioning of Ealing's output from that year on. Hamer was a consummate maverick and at least for a while suited Balcon's desire to test the studio's boundaries of theme, tone and subject matter after the war. Before the decade was out he would go on to direct several more features for Ealing, including *Kind Hearts and Coronets* in 1949, one of Ealing's most popular comedies and certainly one of its blackest. 'Haunted Mirror' is distinctly characteristic of his later work.

Hamer's frequently repeated quote – 'I want to make films about people in dark rooms doing beastly things to each other' – sums up succinctly the pessimistic view that permeates much of his work. The dim light of his world is fortunately sufficient to illuminate the principal object of this story, and a glance at Hamer's subsequent films suggest that his preoccupation with mirrors was not limited to his *Dead of Night* contribution. If, for example, you go looking for them in *Pink String and Sealing Wax* (1945) and *It Always Rains on Sunday* (1947) you will find them featuring, albeit in natural as opposed to supernatural circumstances, as alluring portals to a rosier past or a more attractive alternative present. In each instance there is the strong allusion to a division, represented by the mirror, between a repressed reality and an idealised fantasy. It is a theme and a motif that can also be found in the work of Jean Cocteau; as a *Dead of Night* precursor it is especially evident in his first film *Le Sang d'un Poète* (trans. 'The Blood of a Poet') dating back to 1930 which includes a sequence depicting an artist passing through the 'skin' of a mirror and entering a different reality. *Le Sang d'un Poète* is regarded as the first part of Cocteau's 'Orphic Trilogy', the second part of which, *Orphée* (trans. 'Orpheus') which post-dated *Dead of Night* by some four years, contains further evidence of Cocteau's fascination with mirrors. A particular line of dialogue from *Orphée* encapsulates this: 'Mirrors are the doorways through which Death comes and goes. If you look in a mirror all your life, you will see Death at work'.

The mirror as a supernatural threshold has become deeply synonymous with the horror genre, having travelled far and wide by way of Chinese and Greek mythology, Grimm's fairy tales and the mind of Lewis Carroll. The earliest known mirror myth suggestive of another realm beyond the reflection dates back to 2697 BC, at the time of the great Yellow Emperor Huang Di. It was believed that creatures unlike anything on Earth existed in an alternative world on the other side of mirrors. According to the myth they staged an invasion of the earthly plain in that year and Huang Di used magic to return them to their own reality. The creatures came to be referred to as the Fauna of Mirrors, and were among the many fantastical beasts recorded in Jorge Luis Borges' 1957 magical realist miscellany *Book of Imaginary Beings*.

The Ovidian tale of Narcissus, dating back to 6AD, will be the mirror myth familiar to most, its cautionary tone informing and lending credence to concerns about excessive self regard held throughout history. The Queen's magic talking mirror in the Grimms' *Snow White*, first published in 1812, mixed together similar negative associations with vanity and long held folkloric beliefs about mirrors harbouring a presence on some 'other side'.[11] The mirror through which Alice gains access to a fantastical alternative world in Lewis Carroll's *Through the Looking-Glass* is used as a device for the satirical reversal of the real world but her speech to her pet kitten and initial description of the room that she sees on the other side in the first few pages of the novel is not dissimilar from Peter Cortland's description to Joan of the room that he sees in his mirror:

First, there's the room you can see through the glass – that's just the same as our drawing room, only the things go the other way. I can see all of it when I get upon a chair – all but the bit behind the fireplace. Oh! I do so wish I could see that bit! I want so much to know whether they've a fire in the winter: you never can tell, you know, unless our fire smokes, and then smoke comes up in that room too – but that may be only pretence, just to make it look as if they had a fire. Well then, the books are something like our books, only the words go the wrong way; I know that, because I've held up one of our books to the glass, and then they hold up one in the other room. (Carroll 1871: 20)

The portrait in oils that absorbs the hedonistic sins lived out by the protagonist of Oscar Wilde's 1891 novel *The Picture of Dorian Gray* is referred to in the text as 'the most magical of mirrors'. Although obviously non-reflective in the literal sense, it is clearly still a weird portal of vanity, and it is perhaps not entirely coincidental, considering this discussion of *Dead of Night's* 'Haunted Mirror' story, that a Hollywood film version of Wilde's book directed by Albert Lewin was released in March 1945, depicting Gray the fine-boned socialite standing transfixed before a framed image and inspired to commit wanton acts. There is some physical similarity between Ralph Michael as Peter Cortland in *Dead of Night* and Hurd Hatfield in the title role in *The Picture of Dorian Gray*. It has been documented that Hitchcock was a devotee of Wilde's work, especially *Dorian Gray*, and was also very much aware of the Lewin film version. There are echoes of the Divided Self theme in a number of his films, especially *Vertigo* (1958) and certainly *Psycho* (1960), a film that is famously replete with meaningful mirrors.

In the early years of the twentieth century we had Freud to thank for the formation of the psychoanalytic theory of narcissism to help define and codify the spectrum of self-worship, from surface vanity and the misplaced pride of egotism through to the perils of excessive masturbation and sexual perversion. In the most recent years of the twenty first century we have Facebook and other social media to thank for the recordable rise in Narcissistic Personality Disorder, arguably finding its ultimate expression in the form of the selfie. Illusions of self-worth seem ever more tightly coiled around society's central nervous system, but the neuroses stoked by today's social media pale in comparison to the crises of masculinity associated with the aftermath of the twentieth-century's two world wars, and in discussing 'Haunted Mirror' as a

'I thought you'd like to look at yourself.'

consequence of the 1939-1945 conflict we should look further back to the conditions and motivations of film-makers on both sides in the years after the earlier war.

The German Expressionist movement, so influential on the look and feel of *Dead of Night*, was born of the psychological effects of losing the First World War and the impotent rage of surviving German servicemen returning home to find their domestic role displaced and uncertain. Themes of madness combined with the visual disturbance of disfiguring lighting or actual disfigurement tended to characterise much of the German silent horror films of the period. The psychological impact of a disastrous transplantation in *The Hands of Orlac* (Robert Wiene 1924) and the implications of the surgical punishment inflicted in *The Man Who Laughs* (Paul Leni 1928) are evidence of this, and they were traits that crossed over into the silent and early sound horror of Hollywood. Several Lon Chaney films of the twenties featured amputation and disfigurement of one sort or another and the Universal cycle of horror films starting with *Dracula* in 1931 employed expressionist lighting to frightening effect. *Dracula's* director Tod Browning, later responsible for the dubious exploitation of real physical deformity in *Freaks* (1932), benefited in the making of his screen adaptation of the Bram Stoker novel from the uncredited assistance of Karl Freund, Fritz Lang's cinematographer on *Metropolis*.

By comparison to this visceral response in Germany, the British fascination with spiritualism that flourished in the Victorian era experienced a resurgence in the wake of the losses suffered during the Great War, with many people seeking to make contact with lost loved ones now supposedly residing on 'the other side'. *Kine Weekly*, in its review of *The Other Person*, an Anglo-Dutch production from 1921 concerning a man's possession by an evil spirit, predicted the onset of 'the Spook Era' in British cinema, and while what followed tends not to be widely recognised as a distinct sub-genre, a drip-feed of ghostly films followed between the wars. These frequently took the form of screen adaptations of classic novels, true story murder cases and popular fright fiction from the previous century. Between 1918 and 1939 for example there were multiple takes on *The Hound of the Baskervilles*, *Maria Marten, or The Murder in the Red Barn* (based on a real murder case possibly even more notorious in its day than the Constance Kent case that inspired 'Christmas Party') and *Sweeney Todd*.

In its own unique way *Dead of Night* represents a fusion of these visceral and spiritual responses, galvanised afresh in the aftermath of the Second World War, and 'Haunted Mirror', the story at the literal and, if you will, spiritual centre of the film embodies this particularly. It mixes the notion of a malign spirit on the 'other side' seeking to claim Peter Cortland with ideas of violent, gruesome murder and suicide of which the aforementioned Sweeney Todd would have been proud. When Joan revisits the antique shop in Chichester that supplied her with the mirror we learn from its proprietor Mr. Rutherford that its former owner, Francis Etherington, having been confined to his bed chamber by injuries suffered as a result of a horse riding accident, strangled his wife in a fit of jealous rage before sitting down in front of the mirror and cutting his own throat.

The act that is recounted is consistent with repeated references to other very similar instances of trauma to head and throat found throughout the film. In 'Christmas Party' Jimmy Watson takes ghoulish delight in telling Sally about the violent crime that took place in the country house: 'There was a murder committed here in 1860, I think it was...

strangled him, then half cut his head off'. Hugh Grainger's motor racing accident results in head injury in 'Hearse Driver' and Maxwell Frere crushes Hugo's head to a pulp after 'suffocating' him in 'Ventriloquist's Dummy'. Walter Craig's final act before his attempt to escape through the other houseguests' stories involves the fatal strangulation of Dr. Van Straaten with his necktie and he himself is strangled by Hugo at the very end of his dream, mimicked at the point of waking when we see him back in his own bed seemingly strangling himself. In the final moments of 'Haunted Mirror' Peter's jealousy, precipitated by the mirror's malevolent occupant, drives him to attempt to strangle Joan with his silk scarf. When Joan breaks the spell by smashing the mirror a shard of broken glass causes a gash to Peter's forehead.

These images and ideas of strangulation, throat-cutting, decapitation and assorted head injury fit well as emblems of Freud's metaphorical or symbolic castration anxiety, an idea that emerged in the early years of his development of psychoanalysis. Put simply, Freud considered that the processes of desire, sexuality and fantasy are interwoven with consciousness of self, commencing in the phallic stage of psychosexual development roughly between the ages of 3 and 5, and at this stage the male fear of castration emerges. Freud theorised that symbolic castration anxiety related to feelings of social degradation, insignificance and the tarnishing of pride. In the decades surrounding *Dead of Night*'s release the work of the French psychoanalyst Jacques Lacan was heavily influenced by Freud, but also philosopher turned psychiatrist Henri Wallon, whose 1931 paper 'How the Child Develops the Notion of His Own Body' would prove to be the foundation of Lacan's concept of the 'mirror stage'. The concept, initially relating to the phase in infancy when recognition of the self in reflection begins, came to be applied to the formation of the ego through identification with the counterpart or specular image.

Peter Cortland is an accountant with a comfortable, affluent yet anodyne life. When the mirror enters that life Peter and Joan are making marriage plans and there is nothing to suggest that either party has any doubts about the impending matrimony. Contrary to the rather staid tradition of the Anxious Bride, the introduction of the mirror brings out wedding nerves in Peter not Joan. The story is, of course, told from Joan's perspective; she is the instigator and the decisive prime mover of the piece, from purchasing and having the mirror delivered in the story's first moments to the smashing of the mirror in the dying minutes. She is the socially mobile half of the couple, frequently returning from engagements to find Peter at home, confined, a borderline invalid. Before the effects of the mirror work their stranglehold on Peter his one torpid stab at conviviality – 'What shall we do tonight? Dress up, spend a lot of money? – paints him as disengaged and dislocated. Joan is the potent force in the relationship; in the form of the mirror she is the deliverer of the conduit of lust and desire into Peter's environment, and in the shape of her friendship with 'Guy', her never-seen occasional companion, she is the instigator of Peter's gendered crisis.

'I feel as if that room, the one in the mirror, were trying to…to claim me.'

The mirror is comprised of a central large looking glass with two smaller side panels, and more than once, when the couple are both standing in front of it, we see them reflected in differing panels, divided and separated. Only when Joan forces Peter to confront and challenge his vision of the other room do we see the couple joined together in the mirror's central panel, hand in hand and framed not unlike a wedding photograph, brought into union through Joan's extended force of will. It is enough to boost Peter's confidence, albeit temporarily; in the next scene, depicting the just-married couple in their new apartment, we see him dressing confidently before the mirror with only Joan reflected in his actual bedroom, recumbent behind him enjoying breakfast in bed, reduced briefly to a more passive role. It is a momentary reestablishment of gender conventions; when Joan is mobile once more, away visiting her mother, Peter's self-doubt returns and he again finds himself alone gazing fixedly at himself in the other room in the mirror. He is powerless to counteract what he sees and it takes an intervention from the altogether more powerful Joan to break the spell by smashing the mirror in the story's final scene. She accomplishes this by wielding a decidedly phallic candlestick, an act seemingly orchestrated to emphasise Peter's comparative male ineffectuality.

Google Withers had precious little time in the story to portray Joan as a fully realised, three-dimensional character, and yet during the course of the twenty minutes of screen time that 'Haunted Mirror' occupies she delivered a performance that was the equal of the numerous other 'strong woman' screen roles for which she would later become well known. Joan is confident, purposeful, decisive, and through the implication of her off-screen dalliance with Guy she is both comfortable with her sexuality and prepared to wield it. She possesses what Peter lacks, not just an all-round potency but also control of her own mind. When Peter finally relates his mirror visions to Joan he does so convinced that the problem is of psychological and not supernatural origin. 'The trouble's not in the mirror, it's in my mind, it must be…I'll have to see a mental specialist…it's no use I tell you, I'm going mad!' The torrent of self-diagnosis illustrates both his neutered introspection and also his unwillingness to believe his own eyes. Only Joan's strong sensitivity can break the spell; at the point of asphyxiation, when Peter attempts to strangle her, she finally sees the room in the mirror, but unlike Peter she does not fall under its influence and is able to destroy it. Her actions disrupt his gaze, a male viewpoint that is found repeatedly elsewhere in the film but which peaks with Peter's fascination. Like other male characters, the stare that he maintains is in fact a sublimated effort to look into his own mind.

Anthony Vidler's 1992 investigation of the architectural Uncanny, as the chapter on 'Linking Narrative' attests, focussed on the built environment and paid less attention to the two other aspects that Freud identified in his 1919 essay on the Uncanny: optics and identity, the latter associated with the motif of the Doppelgänger. Freud didn't coin the phrase 'Doppelgänger', that honour goes to the German Romantic writer Jean Paul Friedrich Richter who included the notion of the supernatural double as a portent of

death in his 1796 novel *Siebenkäs*. The Doppelgänger motif, as it came to be defined
by Freud, suggests the paradox of encountering oneself as another, fusing supernatural
horror with a philosophical enquiry concerning personal identity and a psychological
investigation into the hidden depths of the human psyche. When Freud expanded upon
the notion in his 1919 essay he even added a footnote that told of his own startling
brush with a mirror image of himself:

> I was sitting alone in my wagon-lit compartment when a more than usually violent
> jolt of the train swung back the door of the adjoining washing-cabinet, and an elderly
> gentleman in a dressing-gown and a travelling cap came in. I assumed that in leaving
> the washing-cabinet, which lay between the two compartments, he had taken the
> wrong direction and come into my compartment by mistake. Jumping up with the
> intention of putting him right, I at once realized to my dismay that the intruder
> was nothing but my own reflection in the looking-glass on the open door. I can still
> recollect that I thoroughly disliked his appearance. (Freud 2003: 248)

Peter sees himself in the mirror but it is a self gradually possessed by the entity that was
the murderer Francis Etherington – it is Peter but it is not Peter. Optical reflection of
the double as found in 'Haunted Mirror' produces a condition where imagery directly
challenges identity by destabilising the point of view. And herein lies another of the
film's means of frightening the viewer; Peter's stare into the mirror is representative
– a reflection, if you will – of our own stare at the cinema or television screen when
watching the film. This subtly, perhaps subliminally, draws us to associate with his actions,
and just as Peter sees, disbelieves then comes to terms with his view of the other room,
so might we become aware of the immediate surroundings in which we find ourselves
as viewers of the film. Although obviously *Dead of Night* was intended as a shared
audience experience for the cinema there is an added shiver to be had by experiencing
'Haunted Mirror' in a room on one's own. In some respects the most unsettling
moment in the story comes near its beginning when Peter looks into the mirror and
momentarily notices something odd about the reflection. It is a fleeting glimpse for
him and he quickly dismisses it, the viewer sees nothing odd and there's no suggestion
that Peter has begun to see the other room in any detail, but it is enough of a 'corner
of the eye' sensation to plant the seed of uncertainty about the viewing environment
and our position within it. Try watching this story alone and notice how you become

uncomfortably aware of the space in the room behind you.

It may be entirely coincidental, but the very last frames of 'Haunted Mirror', when Joan pulls the rotten remnants of the shattered mirror's frame from the wall, mark the exact half-way point in the film's running time. It is a point of no return; in the minutes afterwards, back at Pilgrim's Farm, Walter Craig misses his chance to take his leave and is consequently impelled to stay and continue experiencing the gathering dream memories. The saving of Peter is the last time in the film when characters 'pull back from the brink' of their respective experiences; in the preceding stories Hugh Grainger steps back off the bus that crashes and Sally O'Hara descends back down and away from the ghostly upper reaches of the country house. Joan breaks the mirror which brings her Peter back to her, but in the subsequent stories it is the supernatural elements that gain the upper hand. In 'Golfing Story' the late Larry Potter succeeds in returning to the land of the living to take the place of his cheating golf partner George Parratt and win the girl; in 'Ventriloquist's Dummy' Maxwell Frere succumbs to the dark psychological forces surrounding him and irreversibly takes on the personality of his dummy Hugo; and in the final section of 'Linking Narrative' Walter Craig makes his inexorable way to the deadly conclusion of his nightmare. One might actually question how complete and enduring Peter's recovery is once the mirror is smashed; while he seems restored and has no apparent recollection of his possessed state of mind, the many shards of broken mirror glass may merely represent the scattering of his still-afflicted personality. Joan is unaccompanied at Pilgrim's Farm which might suggest that Peter is elsewhere still convalescing, not a murderer facing execution, perhaps, but the unhappy recipient of seven years bad luck. Maybe he even went to see that 'mental specialist' after all.

In the earlier chapter discussing *Dead of Night*'s context the mirror was positioned as both recollective and predictive. Peter certainly sees the past reflected in the form of Francis Etherington's lavish Victorian bedroom, but in the breaking of the mirror we are provided with a vision of the film's future. Taken as a designed component within an architectural structure, the collapse of its rotting frame and the fracturing of the image that it reflects foreshadows the folding disintegration of Pilgrim's Farm around Walter Craig during the final leg of his nightmare. In addition, we will witness the breaking of glass at a crucial moment later in the film; the act of Van Straaten dropping and breaking his spectacles is the beginning of his end.

'I'm going to punish you as you deserve to be punished.'

'Haunted Mirror' and 'Ventriloquist's Dummy' share more than the fresh war wound of male gender uncertainty; they both make use of a supernatural vessel that possesses a surface impassivity belying an indefinable 'inner' evil. To onlookers it is *just* a mirror, *just* a dummy; Joan describes the mirror as *'just* a little birthday present' and Hugo refers to himself as *'just* a bird in a gilded cage'. However, as grand embodiments of the Uncanny according to Freud, the Etherington mirror and Hugo the dummy work so effectively by maintaining an outward mask of indifference. Despite their cold, dispassionate exteriors both are capable of drawing the blood of the ones that they latch on to – the cut to Peter's head from the mirror shard and the bite left in Frere's hand by an angry Hugo – and both perish as a result of destructive reciprocal 'punishment' that leaves them smashed to pieces. In the case of Hugo it could be argued that his destruction releases the evil 'personality' which moves to completely consume Frere. As for the mirror, we might presume that the 'monstrously evil' spirit that is released from the glass when it is broken fails to find another host, but Peter's unaccounted absence from the group of guests at Pilgrim's Farm raises questions. We do, of course, see Peter one final time, during Craig's escape attempt at the end of the film, and it is telling that in his dress and manner he seems to have been completely taken over by the spirit of Francis Etherington.

'I WISH YOU WERE DEAD, OLD MAN'

> Unfortunately Mr. Jones' ghost can only be seen by true believers. If you are not a
> true believer bid with caution, for you may be unable to see him. I will not be giving
> refunds so bid with caution as this is something impossible to authenticate and verify.
> (Taken from the eBay item description for a glass jar purported to contain the ghost
> of golf legend Bobby Jones)

'Golfing Story' directed by Charles Crichton is universally considered to be the
weakest of *Dead of Night*'s stories, to the point that its inclusion has been regarded as
detrimental to the whole film. It's quite clear from reading various critics' discussions of
Dead of Night that some, even the most ardent admirers of the film, would cheerfully
drop it for the sake of consistency of tone and quality. This chapter, however, will fight its
corner, asserting that not only is the sequence necessary in terms of pace and structure,
but that it contains and explores, albeit in précis, many of the themes examined in the
rest of the film. What it also does is set the stage for the final, chilling, sequence and
the consequent nightmarish coda which ends the framing narrative. The love triangle
at the heart of 'Golfing Story' establishes the notion ahead of the implied homosexual
polyamory to be found in 'Ventriloquist's Dummy' and in doing so it also echoes the
implicit triangle in 'Haunted Mirror'.

It's a shaggy dog story to be sure, a bar room anecdote barely worth ascribing the title
of urban myth. As a piece it sails awkwardly alone from the other tales told, adrift in its
tone and intent. Unlike the preceding stories, Van Straaten feels no need to even dignify
it with an explanation or rebuttal after its telling. That said, he might have something
to say about how Eliot Foley uses it to manipulate Walter Craig into staying at the
gathering, given his own failure to persuade Craig to stay at this point in the film. Craig
acknowledges it for what it is: a successful attempt by his genial host to keep him in the
farmhouse after he has expressed his intention to leave, to break the cycle of events
before they have a chance to happen. Given the conclusion of the film this admission
is particularly chilling; Craig decides to stay despite his own increasing certainty that
the consequences of not leaving will be dire. In itself this is consistent with the theme
of duty explored throughout the film; consideration of one's host and his kindness
was considered a definite virtue in a deferential era, and Craig's lower social status

established early on enforces this sense of obligation. As a result, Craig's chance to break the cycle of terror is lost to little more than good manners.

The first and most obvious idea worth examining is whether or not the film really would be better and more effective without this sequence. It was excluded from the film's initial release in the United States (along with 'Christmas Party') possibly for simple expedient reasons of running time, and there is no doubt that tonally it is out of sorts with the other tales contained in the film. By the time this story is recounted we have been subjected to mounting dread and a rising sense of incipient evil and ever more explicit violence. The story's narrative lightening of tone before the horror of the final house-guest's story and the merciless conclusion of a recurring nightmare allows us a pause, giving both tales which frame 'Golfing Story' time to breathe. To proceed directly from the actual and metaphorical strangulations of 'Haunted Mirror' straight into the macabre psychological implications of 'Ventriloquist Dummy', from one particularly admired and acclaimed story to another, would risk weakening each.

Of course it requires more than the assertion of a necessary change of pace in order to defend 'Golfing Story'. It needs to be thematically compatible with the other tales, even if tonally awry, and more than just a breathing space if it is to deserve and reward our viewing attention. As discussed elsewhere in the book, there is a great deal of subtext in the film dealing with male sexual anxiety associated with the various threats arising from the War and how these placed constraints on British manhood. 'Hearse Driver' can be read as an examination of a deep fear of commitment and marriage as well as mortality; Hugh Grainger does not want to give up his life as a daredevil racing driver any more than Potter or Parratt want to give up the game of golf. Tacitly, they all know that some sacrifice is necessary for a marriage to work. Grainger is prepared to make this sacrifice in the face of his own mortality. Potter and Parratt evidently want it both ways (double entendre intended, as will be discussed later); their sacrifice, however, means less time spent on the golf course, literally playing the field. The themes of sexual jealousy and impotence, present in both 'Ventriloquist's Dummy' and 'Haunted Mirror', are also addressed in 'Golfing Story'. Potter and Parratt are certainly jealous creatures in their own boyish and bewildered ways and the loss of golf to one or other renders them functionally impotent; the separation from the phallic paraphernalia of golf clubs echoing the theme of castration anxiety hinted at in 'Christmas Party' and apparent in others.

None of this mining for thematic consistency is to deny that there are weaknesses in the story. There are narrative problems with the tale itself; the characters in the other tales at least attempt to remain rational and natural in their responses even if the events that unfold around them have supernatural or horrific elements. They react as we would expect, possibly even as we would do ourselves, whether through terror or denial. The characters in 'Golfing Story' do not behave in a way with which the audience can readily identify; they serve the function of delivering a punchline, much as the characters in a joke must often behave in an illogical or non-relatable way to serve the ends of the joke itself rather than any ends of their own. The story is told second- or even third-hand, being essentially an extended tall tale; the host Eliot Foley is present but peripheral in the story as he tells it, inserting himself into the narrative purely to aid the telling of the anecdote, which sets it apart from the other stories. It is not experienced first-hand by the narrator, nor is it recorded and retold as a result of investigation and therapeutic interrogation as in 'Ventriloquist's Dummy'. We are not seriously expected to believe that the events in 'Golfing Story' really happened, which paradoxically lends plausibility to the film's other fantastical sequences.

Something the story does which the others do not is to serve as a cautionary tale or a morality play. Unlike the other stories, in which the protagonists are acted upon by external circumstance or are victim to unspeakable forces, the story here is one of how to act, one of how to be a 'chap' in the closed male world of the golf club and, by extension, how to be a man in a society hidebound by expectations based on gender roles. Sexual mores were changing, as were gender roles in a country affected by the war years. 'Hearse Driver', 'Haunted Mirror' and 'Ventriloquist's Dummy' all explore notions of individual male responses to this. 'Golfing Story' by comparison takes a broader look at this notion of the companionable, dependable figure of the British Chap in the popular imagination. The creation and maintenance of this figure in the years surrounding *Dead of Night* owed a great deal to 'Golfing Story's two principle actors, Basil Radford and Naunton Wayne.

Radford and Wayne had been first paired together in *The Lady Vanishes* (Alfred Hitchcock 1938), alongside Michael Redgrave, where they portray the characters Charters and Caldicott, a double act they went on to play in several subsequent films. They presented them as an archetype of the specifically English, rather than British,

'We'll play for her – tomorrow morning, eighteen holes.'

upper middle class male at large in the world: solid, self-deprecating and dependable. Ready to do their duty when called upon, they nonetheless came over as essentially comic creations, slightly bewildered by all things non-English and possessed of an assurance of the superiority of their view of the world and their place in it, an assurance which was not necessarily reflective of their innate insights or capabilities. Their main motivation in *The Lady Vanishes* is to attend a cricket match, a desire pursued with single-minded intent, though when the chips are down the chaps stand up for what is right. A chap might be a bit of a duffer, but he is essentially decent and ever keen to do what is expected of him without the mental burden of over-examining the situation and requiring no other motive than duty and loyalty to one's friends and one's country. Forever Little Englanders abroad or at home, existential self-examination is not their strong point.

So by the time of *Dead of Night*'s production Radford and Wayne, both fine character actors in their own right, were an established screen double act. As Charters and Caldicott, or variations of them under different names, they had appeared together in five films by the time *Dead of Night* went into production, including Frank Launder and Sidney Gilliat's landmark propaganda film *Millions Like Us* from 1943. They would go on to appear together in six more films, perhaps most memorably in the quintessential Ealing comedy *Passport to Pimlico* in 1949. Like *Dead of Night*'s other protagonists they have little back story beyond the brief outline of their love of golf and devotion to each other, but uniquely the characters were firmly cemented in the consciousness of British audiences of the day as familiar personas and comic embodiments of sterling British qualities. Naunton Wayne plays Larry Potter, the loser of the bet who walks into the lake, the quieter and more reflective of the pair. Basil Radford plays George Parratt, the more overbearing and blustering of the two; full of brio and bonhomie, it is nonetheless he who betrays the friendship with his act of cheating during the golf game to decide who wins the hand of Mary.

For all the comic baggage of the Radford and Wayne partnership there is a serious undercurrent to the story, one shared with other stories in the film, namely that of survivor guilt suffered by men who made it through the war unscathed, at least physically. The notion of fair play was central to British manhood at the time and this was tested as never before during the Second World War. British cinema had been largely co-opted into the wartime propaganda effort by the Ministry of Information and films made during the war were encouraged to emphasise the quiet sacrifice of doing one's duty in the face of the Nazi peril. Parratt's act of betrayal is more heinous in this light, and Potter's calm acceptance of the outcome and of his fate all the more affecting. Many thousands of British men had played their part in the war and were never to return; they too accepted their fate and had acted in accordance with the obligations of duty. Potter's slow walk into the lake and the poignant image of his hat floating on the surface of the water is a reminder of those gone but not forgotten in the public consciousness. Those who kept their lives and returned often felt that this survival was a betrayal of the sacrifice of their compatriots, that they too should have died and were unworthy of their continued existence.

Parratt's guilt over his actions is given form and interlocution through his haunting by Potter, whose air is one of overall disappointment in his friend rather than anger or bitterness. This constant strain on his conscience symbolised by Potter's ghostly presence threatens Parratt's happiness with Mary; he is undeserving because he survived where his friend did not. At the end of the tale, when the strain becomes too much, he manages to swap places with the friend he betrayed, albeit inadvertently. As a result he is rid of the guilt which haunts him and the desire to allow a fallen comrade another chance at life and happiness is fulfilled. As acknowledged in an earlier chapter, this subtext of survivor guilt is picked up specifically through Hugh Grainger's injured conscience in 'Hearse Driver', the survivor of a motor racing crash who believes initially that he may only be alive at the fatal expense of another driver. Both stories anticipate the theme's extensive exploration in *A Matter of Life and Death*, where David Niven's RAF pilot is the only survivor of a bombing mission which is lost returning from a raid. His story is one of survivor guilt manifested as a contest between Heaven's claim on him as one whose time had come and the love he finds in his earthly existence after his survival.

There are also echoes in 'Golfing Story' of another, earlier, Powell and Pressburger film, *The Life and Death of Colonel Blimp* (1943), in which a lifetime of friendship between the English stalwart Clive Wynne-Candy (Roger Livesey) and his honourable German opposite Theo Kretschmar-Schuldorff (Anton Walbrook) frames the events of two World Wars and the Boer War. This tale of two deeply noble opponents revolves around their pursuit of Edith (Deborah Kerr), who Candy loses to Theo during the Boer War, and explores notions of duty, sacrifice and the emotional and moral costs of war. It also dissects the changing role of women brought on by a world changed through successive wars. Deborah Kerr plays two further characters who appear later, chronologically, in the film; Candy's wife Barbara and his wartime driver Angela. All three of Kerr's characters take an active and assertive role in the tale and alter the trajectory for the two men, helping them to confront the moral codes and assumptions they embodied. The character of Mary in 'Golfing Story' is, in contrast, vanishingly underwritten. She serves no other function than to offer a prize to the competing friends and seems remarkably sanguine about the outcome being one that will suit her. Sanguine to the extent that she is clearly expected to be unperturbed by the switch at the story's conclusion; a heartfelt off-screen scream at the reappearance of the deceased Potter would be quite understandable at the end of the tale, but we don't get one. Of course, this is all of a piece with a bar room anecdote and we are never invited to take this particular tale at all seriously. What can be read into 'Golfing Story's ending is a male fear of disposability and the fate of relationships between men and women during war. We can be certain that many marriages never happened which would otherwise have done, had war not intervened in the lives of people either through death or long separation. In light of this the story has an added poignancy; people made the best they could of the ravages of war and moved on. Situations they did not choose due to world-changing events beyond their control were adapted to and accepted without complaint.

'We can't go on like this old man, she's ruining my game.'

This acceptance is another example of the film's interrogation of Britain's wartime notion of duty and its consequences. Radford and Wayne portray a schoolboy notion of what this duty means, playing Potter and Parratt as not quite fully formed adults, bickering and competitive yet devoted to each other. It is a little surprising that a woman ever managed to come between them. In his essay on the film Leon Balter asserts that the relationship is a sublimated homosexual one. He quotes Freud's idea that 'shared heterosexual attraction between to the same woman is an expression of homosexual attachment between men – defensively disguised as heterosexuality' (op. cit.: 771). As mentioned, 'Golfing Story' anticipates another theme of 'Ventriloquist's Dummy': the central idea of a homosexual love triangle. However the attraction of the two men for each other in 'Golfing Story' seems less sexual than simply narcissistic; as Balter points out, they desire in each other what they see in themselves. They have no lust for anything that they do not already have, the greatest sacrifice that either can contemplate is to give up golf, and were it not for the intrusion of the prospect of marriage this is something they would never even consider. In this light, the golf clubhouse can be seen as the ultimate male retreat and one with a well-documented and inglorious history of exclusion on grounds of both race and particularly gender.

'Golfing Story' is loosely based on a short story by H.G. Wells. 'The Inexperienced Ghost', published in 1902, tells the story of a golf club member who encounters a ghost whilst staying overnight in the clubhouse. He recounts the story as a fireside tale to his fellow members and seems more concerned about the low social status of the ghost on first encountering the wretched soul, demanding to know if he is a member. He discovers the ghost can only leave by repeating a complex series of hand movements. In telling the story he proceeds to perform them himself and drops down dead. The very-much-alive George Parratt vanishes after performing similar gestures at the end of 'Golfing Story' – referred to as 'passes' in the script – though in the Wells short story the hand gestures are implied to be Masonic in origin, adding further bite to a critique of the closed-off rituals of a male-only space. The setting and the denouement survive from the Wells version, as does the sense of the exclusive male preserve of the golf club and the notion that a ghost preserves the innate character of the deceased, echoed in Parratt's insistence that Potter should still remain a gentleman despite being dead, a sentiment that is a little rich considering Parratt's less than gentlemanly behaviour.

In a wider cinematic context 'Golfing Story' belongs partly in a tradition of comedy horror, a sub-genre that David Pirie, in his touchstone study of British horror films, *A New Heritage of Horror*, is keen to distance from mainstream horror cinema. Pirie makes the case that most comic horror films belong in another tradition altogether, relying on pastiche of horror conventions and in many cases a high camp aesthetic that runs contrary to the aims of a genuine horror film. While this distinction has merit, many mainstream horror films consider comedy to be a valuable addition to their toolkit and often include lighter moments as a counterpoint or release from tension.

'I've returned from my watery grave to haunt you.'

By the time of *Dead of Night*'s making the comedy horror tradition was already well established in Hollywood; *The Old Dark House* (James Whale 1932) was a camp comedy of manners adapted from J.B. Priestley's 1927 novel *Benighted*. *The Cat and the Canary* (Elliot Nugent 1939) starred Bob Hope and Paulette Goddard in a more straightforwardly comic remake of an earlier 1927 silent version, itself a black comedy. In Britain, Will Hay starred in the Ealing-produced *The Ghost of St Michael's* directed in 1941 by Marcel Varnel and written by *Dead of Night*'s Angus MacPhail; and from the same year, as mentioned earlier, the Walter Forde version of *The Ghost Train* was infused with more humour than previous screen versions courtesy of its stars Arthur Askey and 'Stinker' Murdoch.

'Golfing Story' only partly occupies this comic horror tradition, however, and does so more by virtue of its inclusion among and in comparison to the other tales in *Dead of Night*. Unlike other films firmly within the sub-genre the story does not even attempt to parody horror conventions. There is, however, another sub-genre of ghostly tales, which are more comedies of manners than scary movies, where 'Golfing Story' might fit more comfortably. An exemplar of this sub-genre would be *Topper* (Norman Z. McLeod 1937), adapted from a series of books by Thorne Smith and starring Cary Grant and Constance Bennett as a frivolous young couple who die in a car crash and return as ghosts. In an attempt to redeem themselves they try to improve the life of a dull, still living, friend (the eponymous Topper) whose antics entail escalating comic calamity before the happy conclusion.

David Lean filmed Noel Coward's 1941 play *Blithe Spirit* in the same year as *Dead of Night*. It starred Rex Harrison and Constance Cummings, and tells the story of a novelist, Charles Condomine (Harrison), who invites a medium to the house he shares with his second wife, Ruth (Cummings), as research for his latest book. The medium inadvertently raises the ghost of his first wife, Elvira (Kay Hammond) during a séance, who proceeds to wreak havoc, killing Ruth in an attempt to reunite herself with Charles by tampering with his car. At the end of the film, Charles himself dies and joins his former wives in a ghostly ménage a trois.

The *Topper* films had a light-hearted and, for the time, risqué appeal, as did *Blithe Spirit*, with Coward's sparkling dialogue never shying away from innuendo. For some reason it would seem that ghostly characters in the days of the Hays Code could sneak a little more past the censor and national sense of propriety than their living counterparts in other films. While the sexual allusions in 'Golfing Story' could hardly be described as anything other than mild, the once again corporeally present Potter's final question to himself – 'Do I make passes…or do I make *passes*?' – before entering the marital bedroom unchallenged by the now-disappeared Parratt clearly signals his intent.

After Foley's tall tale his mother is mildly scandalised that her son should repeat the story in company – 'Really, Eliot, that story is totally incredible and decidedly improper!' – and the ending of the piece with the interchangeable sex partners on a wedding night is unlikely to have escaped the censor's pen in a more straightforward tale. Mary is much more keen than Parratt to retire to bed and consummate the marriage; Parratt's reluctance is as much informed by his awareness of the ever-nearby ghost of Potter, but even without this he seems to exude a schoolboy nervousness and lack of worldliness regarding what comes next. On his return to the earthly realm, in contrast, Potter seem to have a much more enthusiastic anticipation of the pleasures of the flesh and eagerly makes his way to whatever necrophiliac delights await him and Mary, who he clearly expects to be unsurprised by his resurrection.

If 'Golfing Story' can stake a claim to any lasting influence it is arguably on the nominally more serious Amicus anthologies that *Dead of Night* so famously influenced. The Amicus films had a knowing, slightly camp comic feel to them and took from it the idea of deserving punishment for acts of venality, often serving as mini morality plays even if the punishment meted out was horrifically disproportionate to the offence. Despite this observation and this chapter's overall defence of Charles Crichton's contribution to the film it is still hard to deny that 'Golfing Story' is quantifiably, pound for pound, the least effective of the five nested stories in *Dead of Night*.

When viewed in isolation the truth is that it does not even succeed particularly as a work of comic horror. The film as a whole might have been better served with a more vicious and bitter edge to the comedy, the kind of cutting humour found in later Ealing comedies such as Hamer's *Kind Hearts and Coronets* or *The Ladykillers* (Alexander Mackendrick 1955). However, as well as providing a necessary cleansing of our nervous palates between two richly frightening courses, it does make a significant contribution to the film's examination of the crisis of British masculinity in the wartime and immediate post-war period. The themes of survivor guilt and male fear of disposability are touched on, alongside the echoing of themes more fully addressed elsewhere in the film. In particular the love triangle, the sexual jealousy and even the alliterative names of the protagonists find their full and more terrifying manifestation in the next and final story concerning the ventriloquist Maxwell Frere and his dummy Hugo Fitch.

'YOU DON'T KNOW WHAT HUGO'S CAPABLE OF'

> Your success as a ventriloquist will depend a great deal upon your ability to give the illusion of a human personality other than your own. (Edgar Bergen: *How to Become a Ventriloquist*. New York, Grosset & Dunlap, 1938)

There is something profane, idolatrous even, in the concept of breathing life into a lifeless form, an idea cinema explored early in its history. From *The Golem* through Caligari's sinister animation of the somnabulist in *The Cabinet of Dr. Caligari* to Fritz Lang's *Metropolis*, the depiction of an object or body with no anima or animus of its own, but controlled or possessed in an unnatural manner has had the power to unsettle. In the case of ventriloquism the act of 'breathing life' into an object is literal; the voice is the animating agent, control of breathing by the ventriloquist is central to convincing us that the dummy speaks independently. It has been gifted its voice, and by extension its life, but seldom uses it to praise its creator. Misdirection and deceit are at the heart of the craft which centres around the idea of a disembodied voice inhabiting a lifeless marionette. It is this gift of the unnatural voice that helps give Dr Van Straaten's story 'Ventriloquist's Dummy', directed by Cavalcanti, such potential for horror in our imagination. The qualitative nature of this voice gives rise to a cognitive confusion between the natural voice of a speaking person and those sounds which emanate from the object of a ventriloquist's performance in imitation of a voice.

Aristotle referred to this in *De Anima* as the difference between that which possesses or does not possess a soul: 'Voice is a kind of sound characteristic of what has soul in it, nothing that is without soul utters voice' (Aristotle 1993: 32). If we accept the vocal trick that a ventriloquist makes in impersonation of another voice we then on some level accept that the subject of the act is in possession of a soul or a separate persona. As Freud pointed out in his essay on the Uncanny, by quoting Ernst Jensch: 'In telling a story, one of the most successful devices for easily creating uncanny effects is to leave the reader in uncertainty whether a particular figure in the story is a human or an automaton' (op. cit.: 227).

In his book *A Cultural History of Ventriloquism* (2000), Steven Connor makes the case for a long history of ventriloquism that predates to our modern conception of a traditional act consisting of performer and a dummy. He argues that the act of 'belly speaking' receives an indirect mention in the Old Testament through the story of Saul and the Witch of Endor. Sitting uncomfortably as a pagan presence in the Bible, the Witch answered Saul's pleas for help when God would not, summoning the spirit of the prophet Samuel to prophesy Saul's demise. Early theologians underwent contortions to explain this act of sorcery and its contradictions to the Bible, one explanation being that of a mere act of ventriloquism. Later, historical cases of demonic possession and witchcraft were explained, in part, as belly speaking tricks. Before we had a physiological understanding of how the voice works it was thought that these proto-ventriloquists were able to produce sound through some unique organ. The uncanny effect stemmed from the evidence of our hearing counteracting the evidence of our eyes, in a war for our primary senses. An effect diminished, according to Connor, by the rise of technological communications where this disembodied voice became commonplace.

Enlightenment thinkers were to put ventriloquism to use in debunking religious charlatanism or the claims of mediums to speak to the dead, by replicating and exposing the tricks used. The idea of a ventriloquist's act consisting of performer and dummy is a late eighteenth century development, largely confined to fairgrounds, and once the air of magic and mystery began to be dispelled and Enlightenment rationalism was in the ascendancy, the opportunity to exploit ignorance and superstition (along with the need to debunk it) were diminished. As a result the craft transitioned to a form of popular entertainment. This allowed a specific set of conventions to arise, not least being the nature of the dummy and its relation with its operator. By the late nineteenth century the dominant version of the act portrayed the dummy as an insolent little boy.

There is an unsettlingly childlike aspect to a ventriloquist's dummy in adult human form. No matter how the dummy is dressed or the extent to which it has been given the appearance of adult features or demeanour, there remains something of a child dressing in adult's clothes about it, and married with the disembodied adult voice, the effect can seem transgressive. This unsettling effect is heightened by the nature of the voice, which seems inevitably to be in the higher or lower ranges and somewhat strangulated, and further reinforced by the incongruous seating on the knee of the ventriloquist. Conversely, a dummy that is meant to represent a child tends to have a strange, ageless quality with a knowing lack of innocence. The fact that the majority of dummies have an almost familial resemblance in their exaggerated and painted features is also troubling, raising questions about fear of the 'other' being inherent in our psyche.

The rigidity of expression and the mechanical movement of eyes and the mouth, the rictus smile and rigor mortis stiffness do not speak of a living entity - characteristics which Michael Redgrave uses to great effect in the final scene of the story. The movement of the mouth, nonsensical in its relation to the words spoken, is disturbing in itself, an almost obscene approximation of human facial animation. In this sense the dummy suffers from its proximity to the ventriloquist. Where other forms of puppetry can reach great heights of artistry and elegance of movement, this depends in general on the puppeteer being offstage or obscured, out of sight of the audience. The dummy in contrast has a distinct lack of grace and its parasitic dependence on its host is all too evident.

Our cultural ambivalence to the art of ventriloquism found its way into literature early in the 1798 novel *Wieland* by Charles Brockden Brown, considered to be the first American Gothic novel. It tells the tale of a family who fall prey to the machinations of a ventriloquist, Carwin, who drives a family member, Theodore Wieland, to commit murder by making him believe he is hearing divine voices. Carwin admits to being the source of the voices but denies issuing the order to kill, blaming the act on Theodore's own religious fanaticism, placing this tale in the tradition of Enlightenment debunking. Victorian narratives on ventriloquism tended to focus on somewhat more oblique notions of the male ventriloquist manipulating human female subjects, a practice designed to reinforce female passivity and male potency. Look to Henry James' *The Bostonians* (1886) and George Du Maurier's *Trilby* (1894) for examples of this.

A written work much more contemporary to *Dead of Night* and possibly a direct influence on it, though unacknowledged, is the short story *The Extraordinarily Horrible Dummy* by Gerald Kersh, published in 1944. It is a brief tale of a ventriloquist driven mad by the bullying demands of his perfectionist dummy. By the 1940s the narrative of the problematic all male host/parasite relationship between ventriloquist and dummy was well established, through both page and screen. *Dead of Night* was certainly not the first film to portray such troubled partnerships; Erich Von Stroheim starred in *The Great Gabbo* (James Cruze 1929), an early sound film portraying the mental decline of a ventriloquist who can only express himself through his dummy. In a more matter-of-fact portrayal of a ventriloquist Lon Chaney played 'Echo' in *The Unholy Three*, Tod Browning's 1925 silent film, remade in 1930 with sound and again starring Chaney, about the crime spree of three ex-sideshow performers. However these earlier films did not carry the suggestion that the dummy's agency was in any way supernatural in origin. In cinema that idea began with *Dead of Night*.

Several subsequent horror films took their lead from *Dead of Night* in having a demonic or supernatural aspect to the dummy, although none proved as effective. 1964's *Devil Doll* (1964), directed by Lindsay Shonteff, concerned an evil ventriloquist, the Great Vorelli, and his dummy attempting to steal the millions of a wealthy heiress. Unlike 'Ventriloquist's Dummy' in *Dead of Night*, where the origin of the dummy's possession is left ambiguous, it is explicitly made clear in the plot of *Devil Doll* that the dummy is possessed by the spirit of a stage assistant who died onstage at Vorelli's own hand. The story ends with Vorelli speaking in the voice of the dummy, also called Hugo, and Hugo possessing Vorelli's voice. Shonteff was keen to distance his film from comparisons to *Dead of Night*, though there is a direct link through John Croydon, an associate producer on *Dead of Night*, who brought the property to the producer's attention in the form of rights to a short story by Frederick E. Smith. It was Smith who named the dummy in his 1951 story 'Hugo', surely in a nod to *Dead of Night*, released just six years earlier. Attenborough's 1978 film *Magic* also ends with a variation of a ventriloquist protagonist speaking in a voice that is not his own. Neither of these takes on the material is as successful as *Dead of Night*, but they are not without merit, with Anthony Hopkins' sweaty performance in *Magic* being especially memorable. Hopkins plays Corky, whose dummy 'Fats' embodies sexual jealousy and goads his human counterpart into murder before becoming the dominant personality in the coupling.

Arguably the most successful filmed works influenced by Cavalcanti's story were on television, where several notable interpretations of the trope appeared in widely syndicated shows such as *The Twilight Zone* and *Tales from the Crypt*. The 1964 *Twilight Zone* episode 'Caesar and Me' was a memorable addition to the canon and the 1990 *Tales from the Crypt* entry 'The Ventriloquist's Dummy' veered into a gruesomely comic take on Cronenberg-style body horror. *Alfred Hitchcock Presents* dwelt on the dummy theme twice; 'And So Died Riabouchinska' from 1956 featured a fine, heartbreaking performance from Claude Rains, and 'The Glass Eye' from 1957 was a moving study of loneliness and self-deception.

'Ventriloquist's Dummy', if read as a story of a psyche at war with itself, anticipates a rich seam of cinematic material to come. In particular the similarities to *Psycho* are striking in the way the darker alter ego of 'Mother' in Hitchcock's film is channelled through a form of performance distancing the disturbing, dominant and more lethal persona from the fragile and fractured one. Frere and *Psycho*'s Norman Bates share a good deal. Both articulate a distrust of psychiatry; Bates' brief 'madhouse' rant to Marion Crane is enough to indicate that he has 'seen inside one of those places', while Frere displays nothing short of contempt for Van Straaten when the psychiatrist first meets the ventriloquist. 'You want to psychoanalyse me, don't you?' he counters defensively, 'want to look inside my brain and see how the wheels go round…dissect me like a guinea pig, then show me off to your distinguished colleagues as an interesting case…you're wasting your time Doctor, I'm not mad'. When we first see Frere performing at Chez Beulah he encounters Kee initially as an audience member and in reference to Kee Hugo uses the phrase 'trick cyclist', intended as a humorous corruption of the word 'ventriloquist', although it is more commonly recognised as a mocking malapropism for 'psychiatrist'. In *Psycho* we last see Norman Bates in a cell, wrapped in a blanket and completely consumed by the 'Mother' part of his personality. He looks up at us and briefly we see the bared teeth and hollow eye sockets of Mrs. Bates' preserved corpse superimposed over his features. Our last sight of Maxwell Frere shows him in his sanatorium bed, speaking in Hugo's voice, an image that dissolves to leave just his eyes, large and fixed, denoting the final victory of his Hugo half.

The theme of possession is at odds with the more rational psychiatry-based take on the story. Is the entirety of 'Ventriloquist's Dummy' explicable in rational terms or is it in fact a wholly supernatural tale of possession? No backstory is given for Frere's relationship with Hugo, no hint of him being purchased from a shady dealer in demonic artefacts or handed down from another ventriloquist. If a Faustian pact has been made we are not party to it. They are a fully formed dysfunctional couple when we meet them in pre-war Paris, a setting which establishes the itinerant, impermanent existence of a jobbing performer, echoing director Cavalcanti's own time there prior to his move to England. Frere and Hugo have gained a little notoriety as an act at Chez Beulah, run by a black American nightclub singer, the eponymous Beulah, played by Elisabeth Welch.[12] Paris is a revealing setting; many black American performers moved there to escape the overt colour bar in their own country to one which, while not free of racism, proved less limiting to their careers. This small but intended sub-narrative on race also serves as analogous to the outsider status of homosexuality at the time.

The central relationship in 'Ventriloquist's Dummy' has come to be regarded as a metaphorical homosexual love triangle.[13] If we read the 'courtship' of Frere by Kee as being indirectly enacted through his interest in Hugo, it is straightforward enough. What makes the theme more compelling is Frere's tortured jealousy of his Hugo persona. Frere's use of Hugo as an avatar is as much an attempt to distance himself from repellent urges and regrettable personality traits, as it is a ploy to keep Kee at bay. Through this he creates an object of which he is, perversely, intensely jealous.

Kee is a suitor without guile; his manner is masculine, confident and direct – stereotypically American. Frere's brittle, nerve-wracked persona hides behind the obnoxious Hugo proxy in an attempt to sabotage Kee's advances but the thought of losing Hugo is as terrifying to him as Hugo himself is. Kee is explicitly wooing Frere, there is no sense that Kee covets Hugo; he regards the Hugo side of the personality as simply an act – an expression of Frere's talent as a performer. For Kee this talent is the desirable aspect of Frere. Frere's warning to Kee – 'you don't know what Hugo's capable of' (he knows only too well, or at very least fears, what he *himself* is capable of) – can be read as a rare display of professional confidence, which is downright flirtatious given Frere's reticence. As the object of this wooing, though, the insecure Frere fears that the Hugo aspect of his nature is what attracts Kee.

This insecurity as the object of another's affection, of being unworthy of love, manifests through his attempts to sabotage and deflect Kee's advances. The fear that Kee prefers the Hugo part of him indicates his fragile sense of self. At the same time the increasingly strident demands by Hugo to be 'rescued' by Kee can be read as proxy cries by Frere to be saved and made whole. This is reinforced by the absence of Kee's alter ego, his own dummy 'Fancy Pants'. Kee is *de facto* a single person, but more importantly he is a *whole* person, a complete psyche. This in turn leads to a further source of anxiety for Frere; Kee is to him, in all his healthy confidence, an unattainable ideal as much as an object of

'I say, Sylvester, how'd you like to work with me?'

desire. Kee embodies a state of being to which Frere aspires. His own wooing of Kee through the proxy of Hugo veers into the dummy's transatlantic drawl, expressing this longing to be more like his American admirer.

We learn from the on-screen date of Kee's witness statement that the story takes place in 1938, but from the perspective of a post-war audience there is a distinct sense of the shifting relationship between American and British society and how this was altered by the war years, a period when British citizens had a chance to mix freely with American military personnel based in Britain. Kee is a brash, loud American, sure of himself and his place in the world. He has a showman-like swagger and a confident expectation of a warm welcome wherever he goes. He is also kindly and considerate, and reluctantly but gamely agrees to a supervised visit to his assailant in the hospital. His 'war wounds' are evidenced by the bandaged arm that resulted from Frere's attempt to kill him. The shared trauma of the Second World War embodied in this scene affected the respective national psyches in different ways; the United States emerged as the dominant force in the world, a position long held by Britain. As the more damaged partner, devastated by bombing and crippled by the expense of war, Britain found itself beholden to the more wealthy and dynamic United States, in need of its support in the following decades to help rebuild its infrastructure and redefine its society and place in the world.

In contrast to Kee's relatively alpha male 'Yank' confidence, Frere is British male sexual anxiety personified, all emotion repressed to the point of breaking. His discomfort and uncertainty of his own place in the world are a direct opposite of the worldly and gregarious Kee. At a time when global power and influence was shifting decidedly from Britain's fading empire to the dynamism of what was to become the American century, British audiences in 1945 would have had an ambivalent attitude despite the debt owed to the sacrifice of American soldiers in Europe's theatre of war. As noted, Hugo is ventriloquised with a cod American accent and is boorish, insensitive and crude as well as manipulative and selfish. This suggests a longing for escape from British reticence and class-bound politeness as much as it does a suspicion and resentment of the now dominant former colony. The diffident and reserved Frere, with his fragile sense of self, envies his aggressive and unrestrained alter ego. If there is a national battle for identity being played out in the relationship between Kee and Frere then Hugo is an external manifestation of one side of a national psyche at war with itself.

In *Typical Men*, Andrew Spicer defines Maxwell Frere as an example of the 'Post-war Psychotic' (op. cit.: 175-6) in his taxonomy of damaged males. While acknowledging the homosexual aspect of the story, Spicer regards Hugo as an embodiment of long repressed parts of the male British psyche, those that yearned for licence to dominate and bully and to display sexual provocation to women. Further to this suppressed urge to be the typical 'Gainsborough' male, Hugo articulates a trait that the conventional requirement of national sacrifice had effectively negated, namely unfettered personal ambition. The raw, selfish urge to throw aside all sense of duty and obligation and pursue naked self-interest finds its most strident voice in Hugo's final, taunting rejection of Frere in their last shared scene.

In this light Hugo anticipates the character of Narcy, played by Griffith Jones, in Cavalcanti's later film, *They Made Me a Fugitive* (1947), which explored the seedy underworld of a post-war London corrupted by the effects of war. Narcy is an immoral exploiter and manipulator of people, ruthlessly mining opportunity for advancement

'Say, who runs this act anyway? This fellow's almost human.'

without any notion of obligation to others. He pulls people into his orbit in order to use them to his own ends, including the disillusioned RAF officer, Clem, played by Trevor Howard. Narcy, short for 'Narcissus', covets what he regards as Clem's officer class sophistication; Clem in turn is cynically disaffected by the indifference of society to his wartime sacrifice. The parasitic Narcy and the traumatised Clem mirror the destructive relationship between Hugo and Frere. *They Made Me a Fugitive* gives full vent to the expressionistic, film-noir look of 'Ventriloquist's Dummy'. It is also a brutal film, echoing the shocking violence with which Frere physically destroys Hugo.

Cavalcanti seems, possibly as a result of his outsider status, to have spotted a capacity in the British character for vicious and sudden displays of savagery. His 1942 film *Went the Day Well?* is notable for many things, not least the brutality that the seemingly restrained villagers in the film are capable of and the surprise and alacrity with which it can manifest. Taken together, *Went the Day Well?*, 'Ventriloquist's Dummy' and *They Made Me a Fugitive* paint a disturbing picture of a barely suppressed urge toward violence in the British national character. Frere's readiness to turn to violence, first against Kee and then through his suicidal killing of Hugo, gives the lie to his passive deference and acceptance of ongoing duty, perhaps embodying something the British were unwilling to acknowledge in themselves at this time.

'Ventriloquist's Dummy' turns on a memorable performance by Michael Redgrave. He was possessed of a particularly British type of male beauty; he was tall and had a somewhat haughty, reserved demeanour when photographed which belied his considerable range as an actor. Redgrave was a man who fought his own non-supernatural demons throughout his life; he struggled with alcoholism and was bisexual at a time when society turned its face against homosexuality, which was then punishable by prison. Whether or not this informed his tortured performance in *Dead of Night*, it remains a masterful portrayal of a disintegrating personality, especially given the brevity of the actual story.

Redgrave's earliest screen role, as Gilbert Redman in Hitchcock's *The Lady Vanishes*, offers a different view of British manhood, one more attuned to the inter-war years. Here the hero is a more playful, confident but self-deprecating character more at ease with the world, and with a detached and amused perspective on unfolding events. His sense of loyalty and duty is focussed on helping his love-interest in her mission, and his capacity for self-reflection gives an ironic perspective on his own actions and motivations. The role of Maxwell Frere would have shocked audiences who knew him from his debut in *The Lady Vanishes* and his subsequent examinations of masculine responses to the demands of a time of conflict. Frere is a man uncomfortable in his own skin in the very tangible sense that he is not sure who actually inhabits it. With no back story to rely on, Redgrave presents with great economy a man clearly at the end of his tether, clinging to sanity, his remaining sense of self expressed by his desperate attempt to continue in his duty to perform, and to the stiff upper lip which as a ventriloquist is so much more than symbolically essential.

On first encountering him, as a prisoner during his first interview with Van Straaten, he is initially calm and composed but as the conversation continues he begins to compulsively wring his hands, with neither a dummy nor a drink to occupy them. His reaction to discovering who Van Straaten is causes him to refer to the psychiatrist in anxious excitement as a 'brain specialist', a call back to a line in *The Lady Vanishes* where

'You dirty, thieving swine!'

Gilbert Redman first meets the renowned brain surgeon Dr. Hartz (Paul Lukas) and uses the same phrase to refer to him, on that occasion in a deferential manner. In the last scene between ventriloquist and dummy we first see a seated Frere from behind, his arm held in rictus position as if feeling for a phantom limb or searching for the amputated part of his psyche. He is frozen and speechless until Hugo is brought in at the behest of Van Straaten in attempt to shake him out of his torpor and confront his crime. His initial horror at seeing Hugo gives way to desperate cajoling when Hugo threatens to leave him. This is the first time we see Hugo and Frere interact alone; Frere is oblivious to the presence of Van Straaten at the cell door, his back to his 'audience'. The careful ambivalence regarding whether this is a tale of madness or possession is retained through to the end, with Redgrave, as he has throughout, maintaining the barely perceptible movement of his mouth whenever Hugo speaks, even when venting his jealous rage by smothering the dummy with a pillow.

Redgrave's preparation for the role was meticulous; he was already fascinated by ventriloquist acts, often booking them for children's parties which would have given him ample opportunity to study the craft up close. He also admired the performance of Erich von Stroheim in *The Great Gabbo* (1929), and it was this, along with his fascination with ventriloquism, which persuaded him to take the part. He eschewed any wire trickery in his scenes with Hugo, instead working hard at the interaction with the dummy. The actress Diana Graves, a friend from Redgrave's days at the Old Vic, helped him with the delicate timing required for the convincing interaction with Hugo and also with Hugo's voice, a vital element in the effectiveness of the portrayal given that Hugo is essentially a separate character. Redgrave also sought advice from the prominent ventriloquist Peter Brough, later of *Educating Archie* fame, on how to develop the right personality for Hugo.

Intriguingly, another source of inspiration, for both performance and characterisation, could have been Noel Coward, with whom Redgrave had a relationship that started in 1941. In the mid-1930s Coward saw American ventriloquist Edgar Bergen's act with his dummy 'Charlie' at a party given by the socialite Elsa Maxwell, during Bergen's break out of Vaudeville into the supper club circuit at Chez Paree in Chicago. The act featured Charlie's resounding rejection of Bergen and insistence that he could get by just fine without him. Charlie then rounded on the audience, calling them 'a disgrace to civilisation'. Coward was to complement Bergen on his material, and it was on his recommendation that Bergen won his next booking, in Manhattan, leading to his future fame and success. Bergen had chosen to dress himself and Charlie in white tie and tails when making the transition from Vaudeville. Combined with the dominant and hostile turn by the ebullient Charlie, Bergen's shy personality and the proximity of the club's name 'Chez Paree' to 'Chez Beulah' in Paris, it is tempting to see this story passing from Coward to Redgrave and into the film itself.

Amid the British and American rivalry embodied by Frere and Kee in 'Ventriloquist's Dummy' we have Dr. Van Straaten, the teller of the story, whose European intellectualism provides a third contrasting cultural persona. Erudite, logical and sceptical, he provides Enlightenment rationalism in contrast to the repressed sexual urges and manifest violence shown by Frere and the confident two-fisted bluster of Kee. Within the confines of his own story he is very much the outsider, a status that is consistent with his position in and contribution to the social gathering at Pilgrim's Farm throughout 'Linking Narrative'. On the face of it he makes for an odd guest among the Home Counties set. The surname is Dutch, though the accent is German, and we can reasonably make the assumption, given his presence as a guest at a house party in Kent in 1945, that the Doctor was one of many who fled Europe during the ascent of Fascism in the years preceding the war, which would mirror the past of Frederick Valk, the actor playing the part of Van Straaten. The psychiatrist's Jewishness or otherwise is not addressed, though the Nazis' hatred of Freudian psychoanalysis – an aspect of *Jüdische Physik* that they sought to demolish in the 1930s – is well documented. They preferred the more brutal methods of Freud's psychiatric contemporary Julius Wagner-Jauregg, who was ironically denied membership of the Nazi party because his wife had been born Jewish.

Freud advocated psychoanalysis for the treatment of shell shock during the First World War, essentially exculpating the traumatised soldier. In contrast Wagner-Jauregg's approach, favoured by military commanders, recommended cruel treatments intended to force soldiers back to the front line. One of the writers of *The Cabinet of Dr Caligari*, Hans Janowitz, bitterly resented his dishonourable discharge from the German army on psychiatric grounds, though this likely saved his life. He turned his anger on the psychiatric profession, blaming it for his bad dreams, for cooperating with the war machine and turning soldiers into murderous automatons. This anger found its expression in the character of Caligari himself who is perceived as the archetypal 'bad psychiatrist'. *Caligari* played on the idea of dream manipulation and psychiatrist as sideshow impresario. The central character in Fritz Lang's *Dr Mabuse* films embodied the idea of an omnipotent, supernatural villain, able to transcend death to continue his vile domination. Both characters played upon the fear of the unknowable reach of psychiatric treatment, articulated in the archaic term 'alienist' used to describe the profession in stories by HP Lovecraft and Joseph Conrad, a term that survived into the dialogue of films such as *The Front Page* (Lewis Milestone 1931) for the purposes of cynically dismissing psychiatric intervention. When not feared, the psychiatrist was mocked and seen to be as in need of treatment as his patients, a good example being the hapless Dr Lehman (Fritz Feld) in Howard Hawks' 1938 film *Bringing up Baby*.

Glen and Krin Gibbard, in their book *Psychiatry and the Cinema* (1999), put forward the period between 1957 and 1963 as a golden age for the sympathetic portrayal of psychiatry as a profession, starting with Dana Andrews' Dr. John Holden in Jacques Tourneur's 1957 film *Night of the Demon*, a character who barely survives his denial of occult forces. After this the profession largely slid into cinematic disrepute again, with the manipulative doctors of *The Manchurian Candidate* (John Frankenheimer 1962) reasserting a distrust of the profession. The case might be overstated but there is a trend of negative portrayals culminating in the psychosexual violence of *Dressed to Kill* (Brian De Palma 1980), and finding its ultimate manifestation in the figure of Dr Hannibal Lecter. For all his cannibalistic and murderous urges, the warning issued to Clarice Starling (Jodie Foster) in *The Silence of the Lambs* (Jonathan Demme 1991) when visiting the caged Lecter (Anthony Hopkins) is not to tell him anything personal as she doesn't want him inside her head. Somehow, by the time of Lecter the 'talking cure' had become conflated with the sinister machinations of both the First World War doctors sending soldiers back to the trenches and the hypnotic and sinister powers of Caligari and Mabuse. The unfortunate Van Straaten defies the stereotype but despite his rationality he is fighting a losing battle; the film's game is one of setting the supernatural interpretation against the more plausible, though since discredited, Freudian psychoanalytic reading, with the former destined to prevail.

Many commentaries on *Dead of Night* refer to Van Straaten's arrogance and rude demeanour, though this is largely unfair to the characterisation by Frederick Valk, which is certainly impatient, sometimes dismissive but on the whole genial and indulgent given his unrequested role in the gathering as psychotherapist and confessor. What was to become a cinematic trope of psychiatrist as priestly confessor arguably reached its apotheosis in the figure of Father Damian Karras (Jason Miller) in *The Exorcist*. Karras, a Jesuit priest but also a Harvard-educated psychiatrist, sacrifices his life to save the teenage Regan MacNeil who is possessed by a demon. *The Exorcist* is also memorable for the work of Mercedes McCambridge who ventriloquised the demon through Linda Blair; the horrific effect of the unnatural, guttural voice was an instrumental part of the film's success and has contributed to its reputation as one of horror cinema's most genuinely frightening works.

Maxwell Frere might ultimately have been better served by Father Damian rather than by Van Straaten, whose treatment of Frere once under his supervision actually worsens the situation and provides the catalyst for Frere's final disintegration. Leon

Balter praises the film for being the first psychoanalytic movie, and, while not completely vindicating Van Straaten's final diagnosis of Frere's condition, endorses it to the extent that it presents as entirely plausible. Van Straaten's rather regretful description of Frere's condition as 'one of the most complete examples of dual identity in the history of medical science' somewhat obscures the fact that he began his recounting of the tale as one which gave him pause to consider if the supernatural was at play in this case. He testily withdraws this possibility in favour of his preferred diagnosis.

Of course, there is a problem for Van Straaten and his diagnosis, as there is for any amount of attempts to read meaning into 'Ventriloquist's Dummy' or for that matter *Dead of Night* as a whole. In a sense we are all Van Straatens now; while all the analysis regarding the various subtexts about sexuality and repression are interesting and insightful in their own right, there is one inescapable fact which needs to be confronted. Namely, that *Dead of Night* was not, of itself, a determinedly conscious examination of male sexual trauma after the Second World War, neither was it a portrait of the unspeakable and unspoken-of horrors of the wartime experience. It was not made to be defined by its place in the history of cinema or to define subsequent films. Those are the things we bring to it, understandings which enrich our view and appreciation of it and contextualise it, which allow us to dissect and understand the world which created it, and they are no less valid for that. But the film's reason for existing is purely and simply as a horror film, a circular tale of never-ending terror and a nightmare which cannot be woken from. The depressing, terrible end to 'Ventriloquist's Dummy' is not actually one of a fractured personality as diagnosed by Van Straaten, it is one in which the demon wins, a personality is destroyed and possession of the body by a hideously and unspeakably evil entity is the final, mocking victory of the demonic and the occult over the rational mind, which would rather close its eyes tightly and hope such things do not exist.

CONCLUSION: 'SO IT ISN'T A DREAM THIS TIME'

The dialectic of repetition is easy, for that which is repeated has been—otherwise it could not be repeated—but the very fact that it has been makes the repetition into something new. When the Greeks said that all knowing is recollecting, they said that all existence, which is, has been. When one says that life is a repetition, one says: actuality, which has been, now comes into existence. (Søren Kierkegaard: *Repetition and Philosophical Crumbs*. Oxford University Press 2009)

Good evening. Tonight on *It's the Mind* we examine the phenomenon of *déjà vu*, that strange feeling we sometimes get that we've lived through something before, that what is happening now has already happened. Tonight on *It's the Mind* we examine the phenomenon of *déjà vu*, that strange feeling we sometimes get that we've… (*Monty Python's Flying Circus* episode 16, aired 29 September 1970)

The process of writing this book about *Dead of Night* required repeated viewings of the film on our part for the purposes of close analysis. Our wish expressed in the introduction was that a read of the book would inspire either a first-time viewing of the film for the *Dead of Night* virgin or a repeat viewing for the seasoned fan. Some films demand to be seen more than once, if for no other reason than to help one to focus on their component parts, unhindered by plot unfamiliarity, in an effort to see why they were so effective the first time round. However, film lovers revisit their favourite films for a variety of reasons. It may be a simple act of nostalgia for some; perhaps a film reminds them of a rosier time in their lives or possesses a stab of poignancy that they wish to recapture. In this sense a film can become a time machine, a vessel capable of taking the viewer back to a specific earlier experience and permitting them access to the original frisson in capsule form. For others it is more habitual, even ritualistic; 'Christmas wouldn't be Christmas without *The Wizard of Oz*' might represent an example of this sentiment. More than mere nostalgia, it is a 'same time next year' regard for films that harks back but also projects forward, suggesting that it would be almost inconceivable for all future occasions to lack a viewing of said film.

In the case of horror film lovers – that's us as well as you – we would contend that the practice of re-watching favoured films periodically is an attempt on our part to re-experience the fright of the first time. Rarely, though, will a horror film pack quite the same intensity of scares on a second, third of fourth screening compared to the first occasion, or at least our memories of it, so sometimes we go back to the scary movies of our youth and ride the ghost train again just to reveal to our all-grown-up selves how much *less* scared we are now than we were then. Nostalgia for horror is a little problematic; in general terms nostalgic reminiscence of films is usually warm, frequently sentimental, perhaps wistful and typically involve a fondness for the subject. While, after a fashion, we can certainly be fond of our favourite horror films, the feelings that we try to retrace when we go back to them are by definition cold, chilling. They are also contextual; for many of us horror films were the illicit crossing points of our adolescence, and as we grow older and further away from those formative times it gets harder and harder to be scared by the things that scared us back then. Not that it stops us trying.

Dead of Night is a special case. It is all about the horrible inevitability of repetition, and its chills rely on dread anticipation of an unavoidable fate. Walter Craig can only wait, interred within the cramped confines of Pilgrim's Farm, as the pieces of his dream gradually become clearer to him. And there is something in his trapped inertia that strikes a chord with the attentive stationary viewer of the film. Craig and the other tale-tellers find themselves frequently struck static, immobilised and barely able to believe their eyes, convinced that they must be losing their minds. In the intellectual skirmish between Van Straaten and Craig, between rationality and superstition, certainty and uncertainty, it is the superstitious murderer Craig who 'wins'. Having entered the picture with him we are his travelling companions throughout and as a result we are invited to share a little of his madness. The stark difference between us and Craig is that when the dream cycle begins again we aren't mildly puzzled and unsettled by the strange familiarity of the unfolding events – we absolutely know what's coming and have to contemplate the prospect of existing in a never-ending nightmare. Ultimately the peculiarity, spookiness and psychological disturbances of the film's interspersed episodes pale compared to the horror of inescapable repetition found in Craig's own story.

At seventy years of age one might expect the film to have lost some of its power to frighten; its experiential slipcase of cut-glass Home Counties accents and mid-century social and sexual mores may date it for today's audiences, but we would contend that few horror films in the intervening years have achieved its levels of sustained creepiness and the psychological potency of its pay-off. If you should happen to see *Dead of Night* for the first time as a result of reading this book we feel sure that it won't be long before you feel the urge to repeat the experience, to submit yourself to the feeling of being trapped forever in a dream. Maybe next time it will all turn out different. Perhaps Craig will respond to his extraordinary feeling upon arrival at the farm and 'turn and run for it'. Perhaps, after the telling of 'Haunted Mirror', he will 'act on the warning' as he initially intends and leave instead of doing the decent thing and staying to listen to his host's story about his golfing chums. Perhaps when he wakes up from his dream back at home in London the coin he tosses will come down tails and he will choose not to go.

But, alas, we have a horrible feeling that you will find yourself there, on a quiet, sunlit, tree-lined lane in the heart of the Kent countryside, where a handsome Sunbeam-Talbot 10 cabriolet, registration EYY260, will slowly pull to a halt. Its sole occupant, architect Walter Craig, will glance across at the timbered exterior and tiled roof of his destination, Pilgrim's Farm, and a look of puzzlement will play across his face. A look that says 'haven't I been here before?'

'Pilgrim's Farm…I wonder why that sounds so familiar…'

NOTES

1. These four BBC screenings of *Dead of Night* were responsible for our own first contact with the film. For the record, and in the interests of jogging any readers' memories as to when they might have first seen it, the station broadcast the film on Tuesday 19th April 1977, Saturday 16th February 1985, Sunday 27th December 1987 and Sunday 10th June 1990.

2. Despite the pressure from government and censor to avoid the production of horrifying material during the war years it was quite common practice at the time for studios to submit scenarios for potential films of a disturbing nature to the British Board of Film Censors for assessment. In the months before *Dead of Night*, Ealing submitted a number of ideas for future films that, thanks to the negative reception from the BBFC, failed to see the light of day. These included *The Anatomist*, a tale about a surgeon associate of Burke and Hare, *Uncle Harry*, concerning a poisoner, and *The Interloper*, an Angus MacPhail-penned adaptation of the 1927 Francis Beeding novel *The House of Dr Edwardes*, which in diluted form would later become Hitchcock's *Spellbound*. If the censor's decisions had been different *Dead of Night* may not now be regarded as quite such a singular work of the macabre from the period.

3. The Head of Ealing's art department, S. John Woods, hired the services of several leading British artists to produce images for the studio's posters. Lesley Hurry's memorable *Dead of Night* artwork was equalled in excellence by illustrations for other Ealing releases from the likes of Edward Bawden, John Piper, Edward Ardizzone and James Boswell. Needless to say any remaining original Ealing film quad posters routinely fetch high prices when they come up for auction.

4. Further evidence to back up this most frequently quoted piece of *Dead of Night* lore amounts to a letter that Fred Hoyle wrote to Sir Harold Spencer-Jones, most likely in the summer of 1952, from which this extract is taken:

I also remember a remark of Gold's relating to a cinema film project that he had in mind. This was to produce a film without a beginning or end. The idea was that all films so far made have a definite start and definite finish; that is to say, although we may go into a cinema 'halfway through' a picture, we still have no doubt as to which point of the film represents the beginning and which the end. Gold's scheme was to produce a cyclical film that one could start to view equally well at any point. The relevance of this to cosmology was his suggestion that possibly the universe was like that.

5. For completists everywhere, here are the details from the English Heritage listed building record for the grade II listed Buckinghamshire farm house that played Pilgrim's Farm in the film. Let us quietly ponder on the additional changes that Walter Craig would have affected if he ever got round to working on the building:

House. Late C17, altered. Rendered and colourwashed, the upper storey with planked timbering, the ground floor with thick walls of concealed flint and brick. Old tile roof, rebuilt brick chimney between right bays. 2 storeys and attic, 3 bays. C20 3-light leaded casements, matching French doors in centre bay, C19 gabled porch with blocked entry between right bays. C20 lean-to to left. Attic casements in gables and rear dormers. Rear has tall gabled staircase projection to centre, and later outshots to flanking bays, the left raised. Lower C19 colourwashed brick wing attached to N.E. corner. Interior has timber framing with long curving braces to first floor, arranged in 5 bays with narrow central bay. Stop-chamfered cross beams; some timbers re-used. Winder staircase.

6. The 'Dutch' in 'Dutch Angle' is a corruption of 'Deutsche', which reflects its extensive use in German Expressionist cinema. The tilt shot is inescapable throughout *The Cabinet of Doctor Caligari*. It was used brilliantly in *The Third Man* (Carol Reed 1949), cheesily in the 1960s *Batman* television series and excessively by directors such as Tim Burton, Terry Gilliam and Sam Raimi.

7. 'The 'lumber room', the phrase that Sally uses to describe the attic space in which she first evades the advances of Jimmy Watson in 'Christmas Party' and then succumbs to a sucker punch from Walter Craig in the final part of 'Linking Narrative', was also the title of a popular short story written by Saki (Hector Hugh Munro). Given that story's use of the room of its title as a liminal space through which the writer propelled his adolescent characters, it seems likely that it was an influence on film's makers.

8. 'The Hullalooba' constitutes *Dead of Night*'s 'requisite song-and-dance number', not that it occupies a whole lot of screen time, which is interrupted at that with cuts back to the dressing room scene between Frere and Kee. But it's worth noting that the song was written by Anna Marly. Born into Russian aristocracy at the time of the October 1917 revolution, Marly spent her early life in France before moving to Britain to escape the German occupation. She was a leading supporter of the Free French movement and famously penned the resistance anthem 'Chant des Partisans'. Marly was named a Chevalier de la Legion d'Honneur in 1985.

9. After being convicted of the murder of her half-brother Francis, Constance Kent served twenty years in prison before being granted release in 1881. She emigrated to Australia in 1886 where she lived out the rest of her life. She very nearly lived long enough to see *Dead of Night*, dying on the 10th of April 1944 at the age of 100.

10. Sally Ann Howes appears to be the only cast member who has gone on record as having experienced something akin to the supernatural events depicted in the film. There are claims attributed to her in Richard Kleiner's 1970 book *ESP and the Stars* which suggest she possessed Extra Sensory Perception and on several occasions in her life she had pre-knowledge of the imminent death or hospitalisation of friends and loved ones. The most notable occasion came in 1956 when her fiancé, the society photographer Sterling Henry Nahum, known as 'Baron', was admitted to hospital for a routine hip operation but died unexpectedly shortly afterwards from complications. Kleiner's book claims that soon after a visit to the hospital, when all seemed well, Sally Ann knew, as though it were written, that her husband-to-be was going to die.

11. The owners of the Spessart Museum in Lohr am Main, Bavaria would have you believe that they possess the original 'talking mirror' that formed part of the real life origins of the Grimm brothers' *Snow White* story. They will tell you that the mirror once belonged to one Claudia Elisabeth von Reichenstein, second wife of Philipp Christoph von Ertha upon whom the Grimms modelled the Evil Queen. The mirror through which Alice steps in *Through the Looking-Glass* is purported to still hang in the five-bedroom house built by Henry Liddell, father of Alice Liddell, in Charlton Kings, a suburb of Cheltenham. It is believed that Charles Dodgson (Lewis Carroll) visited the house for four days in the 1860s and was inspired by the ornate mirror.

12. Elizabeth Welch only has a small part in *Dead of Night* but her contribution to the wider world of entertainment spanned seven decades. She is best known for her songs 'Stormy Weather' and 'Love for Sale', singing the former at the denouement of Derek Jarman's 1979 film version of *The Tempest*. A contemporary of Paul Robeson, with whom she worked on two films directed by J. Elder Wills, *Song of Freedom* (1936) and *Big Fella* (1937), Welch has come to be recognised as an important figure in the advancement of African American culture in the twentieth century. The recipient of numerous awards and accolades in later life, Elizabeth Welch died at the age of 99 in 2003.

13. Cavalcanti, along with *Dead of Night* co-director Robert Hamer, was gay and Michael Redgrave was bisexual, though the extent to which this informed the treatment of the story or the performance can only be a matter of speculation. The treatment of the subtext is necessarily oblique; it cannot be said that 'Ventriloquist's Dummy' initiated the era when British cinema came to address the matter more directly. We would have to wait a decade and a half for the release of *Victim* (Basil Dearden 1961) starring Dirk Bogarde for that to commence.

BIBLIOGRAPHY

Aristotle (1993) *De Anima Books II and III* Trans. David Hamlyn Oxford: Clarendon Press

Balcon, Michael (1969) *Michael Balcon presents...a Lifetime of Films* London: Hutchinson & Co.

Balter, Leon (2010) 'Dead of Night' *The Psychoanalytical Quarterly* LXXIX (3) 753-784

Benjamin, Walter and Underwood, J. A. (2008) *The work of art in the age of mechanical reproduction* London: Penguin

Carroll, Lewis (1871) *Through the Looking-Glass, and What Alice Found There* Available from PDFreebooks.org accessed 31 January 2015

Chambers, Robert W. (2010) *The King in Yellow* Hertfordshire: Wordsworth Editions

Clarke, Roger (2012) *A Natural History of Ghosts: 500 Years of Hunting for Proof* London: Particular Books

Connor, Steven (2000) *A Cultural History of Ventriloquism* Oxford: Oxford University Press

Curtis, Adam (2012) 'A mile or two off Yarmouth' *Adam Curtis_The Medium and the Message* http://www.bbc.co.uk/blogs/adamcurtis/posts/a_mile_or_two_off_yarmouth accessed 31 January 2015

Dickens, Charles (1851) 'To Thomas Stone' in Hartley, Jenny (ed.) (2012) *The Selected Letters of Charles Dickens* Oxford: Oxford University Press

Dickens, Charles (2009) *The Haunted House* London: Oneworld Classics

Freud, Sigmund (2003) *The Uncanny* (Penguin Modern Classics) Harmondsworth: Penguin

Freud, Sigmund and Hubback, C. J. M. (1922) *Beyond the Pleasure Principle*. London: International Psycho-analytical Press

Gabbard, G.O. and Gabbard, K (1999) *Psychiatry and the Cinema* (2nd ed.) Arlington: American Psychiatric Association

Hutchings, Peter (1993) *Hammer and Beyond: The British Horror Film* Manchester and New York: Manchester University Press

Kostof, Spiro (1977) *The Architect: Chapters in the History of the Profession* Oxford: Oxford University Press

Marcus, Laura (1999) *Sigmund Freud's The Interpretation of Dreams: New interdisciplinary essays* Manchester: Manchester University Press

Orr, John (2010) *Romantics and Modernists in British Cinema* Edinburgh: Edinburgh University Press

Pallasmaa, Juhani (2001) *The Architecture of Image: Existential Space in Cinema* Helsinki: Rakennustieto Oy

Pirie, David (2008) *A New Heritage of Horror: the English Gothic Cinema* London: I.B. Tauris

Radcliffe, Ann (1826) 'On the Supernatural in Poetry' *New Monthly Magazine* 16: 145-152

Rattenbury, Kester (1994) 'Echo and Narcissus' A.D., Architectural Design 64 (12): 35-37

Rein, Katharina (2013) 'Sleep(less) Beds: Awakening, Journey, Movement, Stasis' *The Luminary* 3: 14-25

Scorsese, Martin (2009) 'Scorsese's Scariest Movies of All Time' *The Daily Beast* http://www.thedailybeast.com/articles/2009/10/28/martin-scorseses-top-11-horror-films-of-all-time.html accessed 31 January 2015

Spicer, Andrew (2001) *Typical Men: The Representation of Masculinity in Popular British Cinema* London: I.B. Tauris

Tibbetts John C. (2002) 'The old dark house: the architecture of ambiguity in *The Turn of the Screw* and *The Innocents*' in Chibnall, Steve and Petley, Julian (eds.) *British Horror Cinema* London and New York: Routledge 99–116

Varma, Devendra (1957) *The Gothic Flame: Being a History of the Gothic Novel in England: Its Origins, Efflorescence, Disintegration, and Residuary Influences* London: A. Barker

Vidler, Anthony (1992) *The Architectural Uncanny: Essays in the Modern Unhomely* Cambridge, Mass: MIT Press

Wilde, Oscar (2010) *The Picture of Dorian Gray* Hertfordshire: Wordsworth Classics

DEVIL'S ADVOCATES

"Auteur Publishing's new Devil's Advocates critiques on individual titles offer bracingly fresh perspectives from passionate writers. The series will perfectly complement the BFI archive volumes." Christopher Fowler, Independent on Sunday

THE CURSE OF FRANKENSTEIN —
MARCUS K. HARMES

"Harmes definitively establishes the decades-long impact of The Curse of Frankenstein on the gothic horror film genre."
Sydney Morning Herald

WITCHFINDER GENERAL — IAN COOPER

"I enjoyed it very much; it sets out all the various influences, both before and after the film, and indeed the essence of the film itself, very well indeed." Jonathan Rigby, author of English Gothic

THE DESCENT — JAMES MARRIOTT

"James Marriott makes a strong case for [The Descent] being the finest example of the films that revitalised the genre in the early years of the new millennium..." Black Static

THE THING — JEZ CONOLLY

"...an excellent study... well researched, informative ... and intelligently written in a clear, presentable style. Most importantly of all, however, it does Carpenter's once-vilified film the justice it fully deserves." Exquisite Terror

Printed and bound by CPI Group (UK) Ltd, Croydon, CR0 4YY

13/04/2025

14656601-0004